T0318698

Cambridge Elements ≡

Elements in the Philosophy of Ludwig Wittgenstein
edited by
David G. Stern
University of Iowa

WITTGENSTEIN'S HEIRS AND EDITORS

Christian Erbacher
University of Siegen

CAMBRIDGE
UNIVERSITY PRESS

CAMBRIDGE
UNIVERSITY PRESS

University Printing House, Cambridge CB2 8BS, United Kingdom

One Liberty Plaza, 20th Floor, New York, NY 10006, USA

477 Williamstown Road, Port Melbourne, VIC 3207, Australia

314–321, 3rd Floor, Plot 3, Splendor Forum, Jasola District Centre,
New Delhi – 110025, India

79 Anson Road, #06–04/06, Singapore 079906

Cambridge University Press is part of the University of Cambridge.

It furthers the University's mission by disseminating knowledge in the pursuit of
education, learning, and research at the highest international levels of excellence.

www.cambridge.org
Information on this title: www.cambridge.org/9781108813204
DOI: 10.1017/9781108878111

© Christian Erbacher 2020

First published 2020

A catalogue record for this publication is available from the British Library.

ISBN 978-1-108-81320-4 Paperback
ISSN 2632-7112 (online)
ISSN 2632-7104 (print)

Wittgenstein's Heirs and Editors

Elements in the Philosophy of Ludwig Wittgenstein

DOI: 10.1017/9781108878111
First published online: September 2020

Christian Erbacher
University of Siegen

Author for correspondence: Christian Erbacher,
christian.erbacher@uni-siegen.de

Abstract: Ludwig Wittgenstein is one of the most widely read philosophers of the twentieth century. But the books in which his philosophy was published – with the exception of his early work *Tractatus Logico-Philosophicus* – were posthumously edited from the writings he left to posterity. How did his 20,000 pages of philosophical writing become published volumes? Using extensive archival material, this Element reconstructs and examines the way in which Wittgenstein's writings were edited over more than fifty years, and shows how the published volumes tell a thrilling story of philosophical inheritance. The discussion ranges over the conflicts between the editors, their deviations from Wittgenstein's manuscripts, other scholarly issues which arose, and also the shared philosophical tradition of the editors, which animated their desire to be faithful to Wittgenstein and to make his writings both available and accessible. The Element can thus be read as a companion to all of Wittgenstein's published works of philosophy.

Keywords: history of analytical philosophy, scholarly editing, Rush Rhees, Elizabeth Anscombe, Georg Henrik von Wright

ISBNs: 9781108813204 (PB), 9781108878111 (OC)
ISSNs: 2632-7112 (online), 2632-7104 (print)

Contents

Introduction

This book is not about Ludwig Wittgenstein's philosophy. It is about his literary heirs and editors and how they made the books the world has come to know as Wittgenstein's later works. The one philosophical book published during his lifetime (in 1922) was the *Tractatus Logico-Philosophicus*. In 1929, Wittgenstein returned to philosophical writing and created an oeuvre of 20,000 pages during the subsequent twenty-one years. When he died in 1951, the copyright to this philosophical work was passed on to three of his students and friends. Wittgenstein's wish was that they publish what they thought fit. This is the starting point for the present Element. It sketches what happened to Wittgenstein's writings on their journey into the public sphere, from the day of his death in 1951 until the death of the last of the three literary heirs in 2003. Given that their editorial interventions are not always obvious in the printed volumes, the account presented in this Element could also serve as an editorial note to the study of Wittgenstein's philosophy.

The main source for the story presented here is the extensive correspondence between Wittgenstein's literary heirs: Rush Rhees, Georg Henrik von Wright and Elizabeth Anscombe.[1] I have had the good fortune to study these fascinating documents of philosophical inheritance for more than ten years. I wish all young scholars a similarly rich adventure in reading and research.

1 Publishing the *Philosophical Investigations*

1.1 The Birth of Wittgenstein's *Nachlass*

Imagine that you have inherited the papers of your philosophical mentor and have been instructed to publish from them what you 'think fit'. What are your guidelines for deciding what to publish?

Would you try to think about what your mentor would have consented to publishing or would you maybe consult an archivist or scholarly editor who could tell you how to handle your deceased mentor's writings in a professional way? If you choose the latter, would it irritate you that your mentor appointed *you* for the task and not an institution with a professional staff? Would passing on the task to a professional do justice to your mentor's will? By the same token, if you choose to let your own judgement rule, which parts of your mentor's writings should be made available and would your justification suffice? If your mentor is a philosopher of considerable interest, would it be irresponsible *not* to follow the method recommended by the professional scholarly editor? But then again, what does 'professional' mean in the context of your mentor's philosophy?

---

[1] Erbacher, 'Letters', 1–39.

Such were the questions that Rush Rhees, Elizabeth Anscombe and Georg Henrik von Wright were confronted with as soon as they became Ludwig Wittgenstein's literary heirs in April 1951. They were appointed in Wittgenstein's will with these words:

> I give to Mr. R. Rhees, Miss Anscombe and Professor G. H. von Wright of Trinity College Cambridge all the copyright in all my unpublished writings and also the manuscripts and typescripts thereof to dispose of as they think best but subject to any claim by anybody else to the custody of the manuscripts and typescripts.
>
> I intend and desire that Mr. Rhees, Miss Anscombe and Professor von Wright shall publish as many of my unpublished writings as they think fit, but I do not wish them to incur expenses in publication which they do not expect to recoup out of royalties or other profits.[2]

With these sentences, Wittgenstein ensured that his notebooks, ledgers, typescripts and collections of clippings would be taken care of – about 20,000 pages of philosophical writing – a corpus that scholars refer to as Wittgenstein's *Nachlass*.[3]

As of today, the entire *Nachlass* is available in an electronic edition and parts of it are presented in dozens of printed volumes.[4] A scholarly milieu has also evolved, allowing for research on Wittgenstein's writings, their history, the structure of the *Nachlass* and critical comparisons of manuscripts and published volumes. Hence, the story you are about to read – of the posthumous editing that began with Wittgenstein's own wish to have his texts published – is a success story: it reflects a continuous movement towards the greater accessibility of Wittgenstein's work. But as you will see, the process of editing and publishing Wittgenstein's papers was also a continuation of Wittgenstein's own struggle to make his work available in the right way.

1.2 Time Was Short

Wittgenstein died in Cambridge on 29 April 1951. The funeral took place the next day and it was then that Anscombe surprised von Wright with the news that they, together with Rhees, had been appointed as Wittgenstein's literary heirs.[5] In contrast to von Wright, Anscombe and Rhees had discussed the issue with Wittgenstein.[6] Up until three months before his death, he had lived at Anscombe's house in Oxford and worked with her on the English translation

---

[2] Wittgenstein's will, § 3, January 1951, orthography normalized; published in Stern, 'Availability', 454.

[3] Wright, 'Wittgenstein Papers', 483–503; updates of the catalogue have been published in Wright, *Wittgenstein*; PO 1993; BEE; PPO 2003 and on www.wittgensteinonline.no.

[4] Pichler, Biggs and Szeltner, *Bibliographie*, pp. 2–20.   [5] Wright, *Mitt Liv*, p. 158.

[6] Erbacher, 'Literary Executors', 29–35.

of a book he was preparing. In February 1951, Wittgenstein moved to the house of his medical doctor in Cambridge and there he told Rhees that 'care should be taken in what was published and how it was presented.'[7] Being personally instructed or not, all three of Wittgenstein's literary executors were aware that their first task was to publish the typescript they knew Wittgenstein had developed for publication under the title *Philosophical Investigations* – the result of more than sixteen years of writing.[8]

Something else the literary executors knew at the time of Wittgenstein's death was that they should not postpone publishing the *Philosophical Investigations*: in the heyday of Ordinary Language Philosophy at Oxford, the historiography of twentieth-century Anglo-Saxon philosophy was in the making. In this context, many regarded Wittgenstein primarily as the one who had elaborated Russell's logical atomism and then paved the way for the logical positivism of the Vienna Circle. Ordinary Language Philosophy was seen to have the task of working out what Wittgenstein had hinted at in his lectures and fragmentary writings.[9] But Rhees, Anscombe and von Wright were sure that this would be a gross misinterpretation of their teacher's philosophy and they wanted to prevent readers from this misunderstanding.[10] This is why only four days after Wittgenstein's death, Rhees hurried from Swansea to Oxford and, together with Anscombe, took Wittgenstein's typescript to the headquarters of Blackwell Publishing.[11] The director Henry Schollick 'was very keen indeed on getting the book'[12] and he gave Rhees and Anscombe yet another reason to act quickly: scholars had approached him about publishing lecture notes and dictations of Wittgenstein's lectures that had been circulating privately for some time. Wittgenstein's true literary heirs were alarmed and claimed exclusive authority in a letter to the journal *Mind*:

> He [Wittgenstein] desired and planned for the publication of his work, and in his will he named us as his literary executors. We are taking immediate steps to publish a book, left by him in a fairly finished state, which supersedes the works now in private circulation.[13]

If Wittgenstein's will were the birth certificate of his *Nachlass*, then this note is the public announcement of its existence by those who were given the task to care for it.

---

[7] Ibid, 30.

[8] PU 2001, 12–33; Wright, 'Wittgenstein Papers', 57; Wright, *Mitt Liv*, p. 158; Wittgenstein's typescript used for printing has been lost, but a version of it is Ts 227a. See Sections 1.3, 1.4, 2.1, 3.2, 5.2, 6.4 and A.5, A.6 and A.8 in the present Element.

[9] Cf. Urmson, *Philosophical Analysis*, pp. 106–7, 178.

[10] Cf. Wright, 'Intellectual Autobiography', 41; Erbacher, dos Santos Reis and Jung, 'BBC radio talk', 225–40.

[11] Erbacher and Krebs, 'The First Nine Months', 199.   [12] Ibid.

[13] Anscombe, Rhees and Wright, 'Note', 584.

1.3 Preparing the Typescript

Shortly after Wittgenstein's death, von Wright took early retirement as a professor of philosophy at Cambridge. He had assumed the position only three years before, when Wittgenstein retired, but now wanted to move back to Finland.[14] In the meantime, at Anscombe's Oxford townhouse, where Wittgenstein had left some of his papers, Rhees and Anscombe prepared the typescript for printing the *Philosophical Investigations*. Both of them were familiar with the text: Rhees had witnessed its development and discussed it with Wittgenstein since reading the earliest version in 1937 and Anscombe, under Wittgenstein's direct supervision, had translated the latest version from 1945 from German into English.[15]

While editing the typescript for print, Anscombe and Rhees remembered what Wittgenstein had told them on independent occasions: that he wanted the book to include his more recent work on the use of psychological concepts. This was the topic he had been working on in Ireland since his early retirement in 1947.[16] Now, in among the papers, Rhees and Anscombe identified another typescript that they regarded as the latest elaboration of Wittgenstein's work on psychological concepts.[17] Anscombe thought this later typescript 'transcends everything he ever wrote'.[18] They added it to the *Philosophical Investigations* and stated in their preface: '[I]f Wittgenstein had published his work himself, he would have suppressed a good deal of what is in the last thirty pages or so of Part I and worked what is in Part II, with further material, into its place.'[19]

Scholars, among them von Wright, later questioned the validity for this claim as well as the decision to include Part II: there is no written evidence from Wittgenstein that he actually planned the inclusion or even how it might be included, but there is no doubt that the editorial choices Rhees and Anscombe made have had a considerable impact on shaping the appearance of Wittgenstein's later philosophy.[20]

The inclusion of Part II of the *Philosophical Investigations* also reveals how Rhees and Anscombe understood their task, namely, as continuing the work on the typescript just as they thought Wittgenstein would have done it. This understanding also comes to expression in how they treated the actual type-scripts: after they had inserted their last instructions, Anscombe took Wittgenstein's typescripts to Blackwell for typesetting – and thereafter the typescripts were never seen again.[21] This illustrates that Rhees and Anscombe

---

[14] Wright, *Mitt Liv*, pp. 133–57.   [15] Erbacher, 'Literary Executors', 4–8, 14–17, 25–31.
[16] PU 2001, 27–33.   [17] Ms 144. See Sections 3.1, 4.1, 5.2, 6.4 and A.9 in the present Element.
[18] Erbacher, dos Santos Reis and Jung, 'BBC radio talk', 239.   [19] PI 1953, vi.
[20] Wright, 'Troubled History', 181–92; Stern, 'Availability', 448–9.   [21] PU 2001, 8–9.

regarded the papers they had inherited as working material they had to use to finalize Wittgenstein's book. They continued the actual practice of 'doing philosophy' just as they had witnessed it, thus bringing Wittgenstein's book to the publisher in the same way they thought Wittgenstein himself would have done.

1.4 'Free but Excellent Renderings'

The English-speaking academic world eagerly awaited the *Philosophical Investigations*, but there were very few in Wittgenstein's homeland of Austria who even knew of its existence. This is no wonder, as Wittgenstein had taught at Cambridge for more than fifteen years.[22] But when writing, he had stuck to his mother tongue, German.[23] That is why he looked for a translator and wanted to publish a bilingual book.[24] In 1938, however, none of the candidate-translators had delivered a satisfactory result. But in 1946, when reading the then-current version with Anscombe, Wittgenstein was impressed by her ability to render his thoughts into English.[25]

By 1950, if not earlier, Anscombe committed herself to translating Wittgenstein's book. To study Viennese German, Wittgenstein arranged for her to stay at the house of a good friend in Vienna.[26] Anscombe spent several months there and Wittgenstein was also present for part of the time. Both of them returned to England in April 1950 and Wittgenstein moved into Anscombe's house to resume the translation project. It is said that Part I of the *Philosophical Investigations* was finished under Wittgenstein's guidance.[27] But regardless of how far Wittgenstein and Anscombe actually got before his death, the cooperation surely sharpened Anscombe's comprehension of the literary qualities in Wittgenstein's writings. In particular, she found 'a special daylight character: tough, lucid, crisp, lively and serious'.[28] To her, this was a combination of a colloquial language and a high literary style that she regarded as being impossible to recreate in English:

> Good English, in modern times, goes in good clothes; to introduce colloqui-alism, or slang, is deliberately to adopt a low style. Any English style that I can imagine would be a misrepresentation of this German.[29]

---

[22] Klagge, 'Wittgenstein Lectures, Revisited', 11–82; Pichler, Biggs and Szeltner, *Bibliographie*, pp. 20–4.

[23] Manuscripts that contain Wittgenstein's English: Ms 139, Mss 147–51, Mss 158–61, Ms 166, Ms 181, Ms 301.

[24] PU 2001, 19–21.

[25] Rhees was eventually chosen at that time and his translation with notes in Wittgenstein's hand is part of Wittgenstein's *Nachlass*: Ts 226. Erbacher, 'Literary Executors', 7–8, 29. See Sections 1.5, 3.1 and A.6 in the present Element.

[26] Erbacher, 'Literary Executors', 29.   [27] PGL 1988, xii–xiii; Teichmann, 'Anscombe', 2.

[28] Erbacher, dos Santos Reis and Jung, 'BBC radio talk', 233.   [29] Ibid, 238.

Although Anscombe said that all she 'could do, therefore, was to produce as careful a crib as possible', she probably strove for something similar to what she admired as Wittgenstein's 'free but excellent renderings' in the English translation of the *Tractatus*.[30] To have discussed with Wittgenstein the ways in which his thoughts could be formulated in English might have taught her both the freedom and the scrutiny needed for her translation work after Wittgenstein's death. The first results from the learning experience are exemplified by her work on English versions of the remarks that she and Rhees had selected as Part II of the *Philosophical Investigations*.

When preparing the translation of both parts of the book, Anscombe searched tirelessly for ways to improve it, including on the very day the book went to press in 1953. After publication, she continued making improvements by weeding out mistakes for the American edition and publishing a list of corrections.[31] Anscombe's eventual achievement was so convincing that her translation 'has been universally accepted as if it contained the *ipsissima verba* of Wittgenstein'.[32]

1.5 Wittgenstein and Anscombe

Elizabeth Anscombe, the daughter of a schoolmaster and a headmistress, fell for philosophy in her youth, after reading a book called *Natural Theology* by a nineteenth-century Jesuit.[33] In 1937, at the age of eighteen, she began studying classics and philosophy at St Hugh's College in Oxford.[34] Her extraordinary capacity for grappling with philosophical questions was already evident in her final exam but it was only later, in Wittgenstein's classes, that she experienced the 'extraction', as she put it, of the 'central nerve' of her original philosophical puzzlements.[35] Wittgenstein, in turn, valued Anscombe and considered her to be one of the best students he had ever had.[36]

Having received a studentship from Newnham College, Cambridge, Anscombe attended most of the lectures Wittgenstein gave after he returned from a prolonged leave of absence during World War II and she met with him for philosophical discussion outside class. Then Anscombe started to learn German, as she remembered:

> I told Wittgenstein, and he said 'Oh, I am very glad, for if you learn German, then I can give you my book to read.' This had been my hope, and it spurred

---

[30] Anscombe, *Wittgenstein's Tractatus*, p. 17.

[31] Anscombe, 'Letter to von Wright', 17 May 1953; Anscombe, 'Note on the English Version', 521–2.

[32] Kenny, 'Brief History', 342.   [33] Anscombe, *Metaphysics*, p. VII.

[34] Teichmann, *Philosophy of Anscombe*, pp. 1–9.   [35] Anscombe, *Metaphysics*, pp. xiii–ix.

[36] WC 2012, 374.

me on. We read the introduction to Frege's *Grundlagen* together. He professed amazed admiration at my laying hold of the construction of the sentences. He said, what no doubt was true, that it must have been the fruit of a training in Latin. But I was struck by the incongruousness of his admiring the exercise of so elementary a skill, which I thought a very slight display of intelligence, when one could get into fearful trouble in his lectures for not grasping something which I was sure it needed great powers and hard thought to grasp. We eventually read the early part of the *Investigations*; I remember he reacted with real pleasure when I told him that I had read to §35 and had found it intoxicating; which was the case. As we read it we discussed translating it – he would explain the import of words, and I would suggest an English rendering, about which he would be very enthusiastic.[37]

When Wittgenstein retired early in 1947, Anscombe continued to discuss and work with him.[38] She understood that Frege's work was not merely one influence among others, but had to be recognized as *the* historical background of the *Tractatus* and that the Frege-oriented reading of the *Tractatus* provided the background for understanding the *Philosophical Investigations*.[39] Later, she championed this reading and put it in the context of the *longue durée* of the history of philosophy. For her, Wittgenstein was a truly great philosopher – on a par with the greatest philosophers of the past.[40] As she told her daughter, it was only through walking and talking with him that she recognized the significance of the great ancient philosophers.[41] Her early writings bear witness of how she let, for instance, Parmenides's or Aristotle's questions mingle with her acquisition of Wittgenstein's thought and the philosophical analysis of her day.[42]

2 Perspectives on *Philosophical Investigations* and the *Tractatus*

2.1 The Literary Executors' First Conference

While Anscombe was immersed in translating, Rhees and von Wright began exploring the papers they had inherited, grappling with the question of what could be published next. It was clear to them that *Philosophical Investigations* was Wittgenstein's second great work after the *Tractatus* and that it occupied a unique place in his *Nachlass*.[43] But it was also obvious to them that they ought to publish other parts of the *Nachlass* as well.[44] There were several candidates:

---

[37] Erbacher, 'Literary Executors', 29.   [38] Ibid, 25–31.
[39] Anscombe, *Wittgenstein's Tractatus*, pp. 12–20, 98–112; Erbacher, dos Santos Reis and Jung, 'BBC radio talk', 229.
[40] Anscombe, *Plato to Wittgenstein*, pp. xiii–xx.   [41] Ibid.
[42] Anscombe, 'Reality of the Past', 38–59; Anscombe, 'Aristotle', 1–63.
[43] Wright, 'Wittgenstein Papers', 501.
[44] Rhees, 'Correspondence with Kenny', 2 March 1977, published in Erbacher, 'Philosophical Reasons', 116–7.

Firstly, there was a ledger that apparently stemmed from the first year of Wittgenstein's return to philosophical writing in 1929.[45]

Secondly, Rhees, who was also heir to Wittgenstein's library, received from Trinity College a box that he expected to contain some of Wittgenstein's books. Yet when he opened the box in December 1951, he found a number of small notebooks and larger ledgers written in Wittgenstein's hand.[46] Then he recalled that Wittgenstein 'used to carry the smaller ones in his pocket; and some, at least, of the notes he made in them were copied – or revisions of them were written – into the larger note books'.[47] Rhees recognized remarks on mathematics that stemmed from the time when Wittgenstein had visited him in Swansea in 1942–3. But the dating in the manuscripts revealed that the material covered a time span between 1932 and 1947. Rhees was immediately convinced that this material would have to be put into a book, but only after careful study.

Third, the literary executors became aware of further writings by Wittgenstein kept in Austria. Simultaneously to Rhees's inquiries, von Wright began an exchange with Wittgenstein's sister, Margarete Stonborough, who lived in Vienna. Being grateful for what the literary executors were doing to commemorate her brother, she invited them to Austria.[48] Von Wright arrived first in the early summer of 1952 and Wittgenstein's sister showed him notebooks from Wittgenstein's time as a soldier in World War I.[49] Wittgenstein had been a volunteer in the Austrian Army when war broke out, but had continued the philosophical work that he had begun as a student of Russell and Moore.[50] Thus, in the wartime notebooks, von Wright could see the traces of the thinking that had led to the *Tractatus*. What is more, Mrs Stonborough showed him another manuscript, one that was inscribed for her with 'Christmas 1936 a poor present'.[51] But that manuscript was nothing less than a beautiful copy of 188 handwritten paragraphs constituting the very first version of the *Philosophical Investigations*, written in Skjolden, in Norway, in the winter months of 1936.[52]

---

[45] Ts 209 edited in PB 1964, first English edition PB 1975. See Sections 2.3, 3.3, 3.4, 3.5, 4.2 and 4.5 and A.2 in the present Element.

[46] These may have included Ms 125. See Sections 2.3 and 2.4 and A.7 in the present Element.

[47] Wright, 'Correspondence with Rhees', 16 December 1951, published in Erbacher and Krebs, 'First Nine Months', 225–7.

[48] Von Wright, *Mitt Liv*, pp. 175–8.

[49] Mss 101–3, edited in TB 1961. See Sections 2.5, 4.2, 4.3, 4.5, 5.4, 5.6 and A.1 in the present Element.

[50] Wright, 'Biographical Sketch', 531–5; McGuinness, *Young Ludwig*, pp. 204–66; cf. Pilch, 'Frontverläufe', 101–54.

[51] Ms 142, flyleaf.

[52] Ms 142, edited in PU 2001, 51–204. See Sections 2.4, 3.2, 6.4 and A.5 in the present Element.

All this material, although only a fraction of the *Nachlass*, was considered for publication when Anscombe and Rhees joined von Wright in Austria.[53] The three executors stayed in the Wittgenstein family's magnificent Villa Toscana. Here they conferred for ten days and decided that the next book ought to present Wittgenstein's writings on the foundations of mathematics. Since Wittgenstein's ideas on this topic had undergone long development, they began by selecting remarks from the material Rhees had received from Trinity College. This was the first of Rhees, Anscombe and von Wright's many 'editorial conferences' that took place approximately once a year in Cambridge or Oxford.[54]

2.2 Portraits of the Man

Before the literary executors began preparing the *Remarks on the Foundations of Mathematics*, the proofs for the *Philosophical Investigations* had to be corrected. Von Wright helped with proofreading and Anscombe kept on improving her translation until the book appeared in May 1953.[55]

In the meantime, the literary executors learned of even more writings by Wittgenstein. For instance, they received material from the time before World War I, which included a manuscript Wittgenstein had put together as a student and a text he had dictated to Moore in Skjolden in 1913.[56] Von Wright was intrigued by how these works shed further light on the origins of the *Tractatus* and wondered how best to publish them.[57]

Coinciding with this historical interest, the literary executors were compelled to deal with biographical accounts of Wittgenstein. Journal articles about Wittgenstein offered, on one hand, new and interesting biographical facts, but on the other, could distort the picture of the man the literary executors had known.[58] While Anscombe published rectifications of false claims as soon as they came to light, von Wright thought about writing a biographical account of Wittgenstein himself.[59] Then, as if out of the blue, the later Nobel laureate in economics, Friedrich August von Hayek – a remote cousin of Wittgenstein – contacted von Wright concerning his own plan to write a biographical sketch.[60]

Hayek had received chronologies and documents from Wittgenstein's close friends in Austria and England, including his correspondence with Russell that would provide the backbone for his biography.[61] It did not take Hayek long to

---

[53] Von Wright, *Mitt Liv*, pp. 175–8.   [54] Erbacher, 'Letters', 1–36.

[55] Wright, 'Letter to Anscombe', 17 May 1953.

[56] Ms 301, edited in TB 1961, 107–18 (AM 1961).

[57] Wright, 'Correspondence with Anscombe', 1953–60.

[58] Cranston, 'Bildnis', 495–7; Ferrater Mora, 'Destruktion', 489–95; Gasking and Jackson, 'Ludwig Wittgenstein', 73–80; cf.: Ground and Flowers (eds.), *Portraits*.

[59] Anscombe, 'To the Editor', 97–8.   [60] Hayek, *Draft Biography*, pp. 9–26.

[61] The complete correspondence of Wittgenstein is edited in GESAMTBRIEFWECHSEL (2011).

compose a draft that he sent around for comments.[62] But things did not go as he expected; after the literary executors and Wittgenstein's sister Margarete read the draft, they concurred that Hayek's biographical project should be stopped. They thought Wittgenstein would have loathed a biography that dealt with his personal life and was not seriously in touch with his philosophical work. Hence, the literary executors did not permit Hayek to quote from Wittgenstein's letters to Russell before the letters had been published by themselves. They thus thwarted Hayek's plans.

Hayek himself probably realized that the endeavour he had launched into required much more research than he initially envisaged.[63] However, the material he had gathered was of great value to subsequent biographers. Indeed, von Wright himself used it when writing his own biographical sketch shortly thereafter.[64] In contrast to Hayek's draft, von Wright's account was acclaimed by many – among them Margarete Stonborough and Hayek, too – and it soon became a classic of the genre.[65]

2.3 A Proper Picture of Wittgenstein's Life Work

By the spring of 1953, when the *Philosophical Investigations* were about to appear in England, almost a year had passed since the literary executors met in Austria and decided that their next volume ought to consist of Wittgenstein's remarks on the foundations of mathematics. During that year, Anscombe's husband Peter Geach read the ledger from 1929–30, the first year after Wittgenstein's return to philosophical writing.[66] At the time of Wittgenstein's death, this ledger was kept by G. E. Moore, who was supposed to turn it over to Wittgenstein's executor.[67] Moore gave it to Rhees in 1951 and the literary executors referred to it thereafter as the 'Moore volume'. Now, after reading the Moore volume, Geach urged the literary executors to publish it.[68] Von Wright then reread it and concurred that they ought to make the Moore volume their next publication:

> The M-V in many ways represents a 'middle case' between the W. of the Tractatus and the W. of the Untersuchungen. It is often interesting from the point of view of illuminating the earlier work and sometimes also as an anticipation of the later thoughts from the Blue Book onwards. It gets additional interest from the fact that it deals fairly extensively with certain

---

[62] Hayek, *Draft Biography*, pp. 28–82.   [63] Hayek, *Draft Biography*, p. 86.

[64] Wright, 'Biographical Sketch', 527–45.

[65] Erbacher, 'First Wittgenstein Biography', 20–1; cf. Broad, 'Review'.

[66] Ts 209, edited in PB 1964, first English edition: PB 1975. See Sections 2.1, 3.3, 3.4, 3.5, 4.2 and 4.5 and A.2 in the present Element.

[67] PB 1964, editor's note; WC 2012, 435–6.   [68] Erbacher, Jung and Seibel, 'Logbook', 107.

topics on which, for all I know, W. has written hardly anything anywhere else. (Visual space geometry, recursive proof, probability on which, however, he also wrote in the Tractatus.)[69]

But Rhees argued against this idea:

> It often expresses views which will seem to foster current misunderstandings of Wittgenstein, and will hinder an understanding of his later doctrines. Hinder, because there are many, I think, who will lap up these statements more readily than the later ones; and such readers will – or may – not recognize the gap there is between this and his later position, but will think of his later statements in the light of these.[70]

In many ways, Rhees's concern about readers possibly misunderstanding the edited volumes foreshadows the motivation for his method of editing in later years. As early as in 1953, he insisted that they should wait with the Moore volume and instead continue 'carving' from Wittgenstein's later work on the foundations of mathematics, in order to provide a proper picture of Wittgenstein's entire life work.[71] This convinced von Wright, who vividly remembered sitting in class in 1939 and witnessing the intellectual duels between Wittgenstein and Alan Turing.[72] What is more, he knew that it was the philosophy of logic as the foundation of mathematics that had made Wittgenstein turn to philosophizing in the first place in 1911 and L. E. J. Brouwer's lecture on the foundational crisis had been decisive for his return to Cambridge in 1929.[73] Subsequently, Wittgenstein dealt with the philosophy of mathematics in many of his lectures at Cambridge.[74] The literary executors therefore decided once again that the next project would be to edit Wittgenstein's *Remarks on the Foundations of Mathematics*, thus to do justice to the importance that this work had had for their former teacher.[75]

2.4 The Troubled History of Editing the *Remarks on the Foundations of Mathematics*

Even by the early 1930s, that is, before the first version of the *Philosophical Investigations*, Wittgenstein planned to make his remarks on the foundations of mathematics the second part of the future book.[76] He worked at great length,

---

[69] Wright, 'Correspondence with Anscombe', 4 April 1953, published in Erbacher, Jung and Seibel, 'Logbook', 107.

[70] Wright, 'Correspondence with Rhees', 22 April 1953, published in Erbacher, Jung and Seibel, 'Logbook', 108.

[71] Ibid.   [72] Wright, *Mitt Liv*, p. 77; the 1939 lectures are edited in LFM 1976.

[73] Wright, 'Biographical Sketch', 529–32, 537; McGuinness, *Approaches*, pp. 178–79, 190; cf. Stadler, *Wiener Kreis*, pp. 449–50.

[74] Klagge, 'Wittgenstein Lectures, Revisited', 26–82.

[75] RFM 1956, cf. Wright, 'Biographical Sketch', 501–2.

[76] Ts 213, edited in Will and BT 2005. See Sections 3.5 and 5.1 and A.3 in the present Element.

repeatedly revising the text until 1944, the year he dropped any further elaboration on the topic and turned his attention to psychological concepts.[77]

The whole of the resulting written material on the foundations of mathematics appeared to the literary executors to be unready for publication. Apart from a fairly well-composed typescript that had been intended as the second part of the book that Wittgenstein wanted to publish as *Philosophical Remarks* in 1938, there seemed to be no single and clearly identifiable text that could be considered the most finished version. The literary executors therefore started putting together a volume consisting of material from several manuscripts written between 1937 and 1944.[78] They decided that some of these scripts should be included in the book in their entirety, while excerpts would be selected from others. The strategy was for Rhees and von Wright each to type a part of the selected material and for Anscombe to then translate everything into English.

At the outset of the editorial work, however, Anscombe already felt dubious about not cutting down on what she experienced as boring repetitions while leaving out other remarks that appeared to her to be essential.[79] Similarly, von Wright was constantly tormented by the question of whether or not they were doing the 'right thing'.[80] There were also practical problems: von Wright only had poor-quality photos of the manuscripts to work from, so he struggled simply to decipher what was in them and the arduous task of typesetting unusual mathematical symbols seemed to necessitate endless proofreading.[81] In spite of all the challenges, Rhees was convinced that the volume was a necessary safeguard against a gross misunderstanding of Wittgenstein's whole philosophy.

The literary executors therefore endured three years of editing and *Remarks on the Foundations of Mathematics* was eventually published in 1956.[82] But the troubled history of their editing continued. The book was largely ignored by the philosophical community[83] and it received some severe criticism, beginning with a review by one of Wittgenstein's most cherished students, the mathematician Georg Kreisel, who concluded:

> I did not enjoy reading the present book. Of course I do not know what I should have thought of it fifteen years ago; now it seems to me to be a surprisingly insignificant product of a sparkling mind.[84]

---

[77] PU 2001, 19–25.   [78] Tss 221–4, Mss 117, 121–2, 124–7, 164, all edited in RFM 1956.

[79] Wright, 'Correspondence with Anscombe', 4 July 1954, published in Erbacher, 'Approaches', 175.

[80] Wright, 'Correspondence with Anscombe', 2 January 1955, published in Erbacher, 'Approaches', 175.

[81] Wright, 'Correspondence with Anscombe', 1954–6.   [82] RFM 1956.

[83] Cf. Wright, 'Correspondence with Rhees', 4 and 5 September 1962, published in Erbacher, Jung and Seibel, 'Logbook', 114–21.

[84] Kreisel, 'Foundations of Mathematics', 158.

Even today, few people seem to have come to appreciate Wittgenstein's remarks on the foundations of mathematics to the extent that the literary executors hoped to foster.[85] This may partly be due to the shape of the volume, for it is more of a patchwork than most of the subsequent books. In fact, von Wright later regarded it as the one that was most in need of revision.[86] Interestingly, it remains the only volume in which all three literary executors acted together as editors.

2.5 Pre-Tractarian Writings

Anscombe and von Wright's correspondence from the time of editing the *Remarks on the Foundations of Mathematics* typically conveys two alternating moods: first, frustration over the many technical problems of editing, and, second, invigoration when discussing the *Tractatus*.[87]

While typing his share of the remarks on mathematics in 1954, von Wright was giving a class on the *Tractatus* at Cornell University.[88] He had been invited to Cornell by Norman Malcolm, whom he had met in Wittgenstein's class in 1939 and again in Wittgenstein's last class in 1947 (this was when they became friends). Now Malcolm – alongside Max Black and John Rawls – attended von Wright's class, making it an 'exhilarating experience'.[89] Anscombe, in Oxford, was preparing lectures on the *Tractatus* as well.[90] Sharing the fascination of rediscovering Wittgenstein's early work, she and von Wright, in their letters to each other, commented on exegetical questions, and this sometimes even led to energetic arguments.[91]

To shed light on some passages in the *Tractatus* that Anscombe and von Wright read differently, they found it useful to consult Wittgenstein's notebooks from World War I.[92] Anscombe had taken microfilm copies of them in Austria in 1952 and she now shared these with von Wright.[93] While reading and using them, both Anscombe and von Wright decided they ought to publish these notebooks next. Von Wright regarded them as of great value for anyone seriously interested in the

---

[85] A new extensive commentary is currently being prepared; see Mühlhölzer, *Ein Kommentar*, 1–102.

[86] Wright, 'Correspondence with Rhees', 1972–3; cf. Kenny, 'Brief History', 342. A revision of the book did appear in 1974 (RFM 1974 and 1978). See Section 5.2 in the present Element.

[87] Wright, 'Correspondence with Anscombe', 1954–6.   [88] Wright, *Mitt Liv*, pp. 186–9.

[89] Wright, 'Correspondence with Anscombe', 4 June 1954. A list of attendees is kept at the Von Wright and Wittgenstein Archives at the University of Helsinki.

[90] cf. Anscombe, *Wittgenstein's Tractatus,* Acknowledgements. A list of Anscombe's lectures at Oxford and Cambridge is available at www.unav.es/filosofia/jmtorralba/anscombe/.

[91] One *Tractatus*-paragraph they discussed heatedly was 5.62. Cf. Anscombe, *Wittgenstein's Tractatus*, p. 166, and Hintikka, 'Wittgenstein's solipsism', 88–91.

[92] Ms 101–3. See Sections 2.1, 4.2, 4.3, 4.5, 5.4, 5.6 and A.1 in the present Element.

[93] Wright, 'Correspondence with Anscombe', 1954–6.

Tractatus and he thought the same about other pre-Tractarian writings: the typescript 'Notes on Logic', the dictation to Moore and the substantial correspondence between Wittgenstein and Russell.[94] Thus, von Wright and Anscombe included these writings when editing Wittgenstein's notebooks from World War I, which appeared under the title *Notebooks 1914–16* in 1961.[95]

Anscombe and von Wright did not, however, publish Wittgenstein's war notebooks and the additional material exactly as they had found them. Rather, they chose for publication only those parts that they regarded as philosophically relevant. Most importantly, they excluded the so-called coded remarks. Wittgenstein had the habit of writing his philosophical work on the right-hand pages of the war notebooks, while keeping more diary-like entries on the left-hand pages, coding them by inverting the alphabet. For Anscombe and von Wright, it was out of the question to publish these coded entries; this was an act of piety towards a friend. Their decision is fairly understandable, for it concerned private notes or personal comments about comrades.

Today, scholars see that some of Wittgenstein's coded entries do directly illuminate the philosophy Wittgenstein was creating in the trenches and some provide interesting meta-commentary on his work.[96] Being thus aware of the coded remarks' potential significance, scholars have criticized the literary executors' policy not to publish them; but even today, a printed volume that presents in juxtaposition both the right and the left pages of Wittgenstein's war notebooks remains a desideratum.[97]

2.6 Historical Contexts

When Wittgenstein's literary executors edited his *Notebooks 1914–1916*, they mixed historical and systematic interests. This sort of mixture is typical when dealing with the papers a philosopher has left to posterity and each executor had his or her own way of mixing the two interests.

Anscombe wanted the *Tractatus* and the *Philosophical Investigations* to be read according to what she considered to be the correct understanding of its relevant historical context. This was paramount to her, whereas she only regarded bits and pieces from his *Nachlass* as relevant if they directly illuminated the reading of these two main works. She saw no philosophical point in biographical accounts of Wittgenstein (most of which would be bound to be foolish anyhow,

---

[94] Ts 201a, Ms 301, edited in TB 1961.   [95] TB 1961.

[96] VB 1994 and VB 1998; Somavilla, 'Coded Remarks', 30–50; Klagge, *Exile*, pp. 5–18. The coded remarks are available in their entirety in BEE 2000 and online at www .wittgensteinsource.org.

[97] Stern, 'Availability', 460–1. A publication with both sides of Wittgenstein's war notebooks in German and in English will be available shortly. See Section A.1 in the present Element.

according to her) and reflected: 'If by pressing a button it could have been secured that people would not concern themselves with his personal life, I should have pressed the button.'[98] Her *Introduction to Wittgenstein's Tractatus* shows this attitude paradigmatically when she exclusively outlines Frege's work and then announces that 'this then is the historical background of the Tractatus'.[99]

By contrast, von Wright, who had been much inspired by Jacob Burckhardt's cultural histories in his youth, was intrigued by how the *Nachlass* made it possible to reconstruct the origins of Wittgenstein's great works.[100] He found it fascinating to trace the history of the *Tractatus* and the *Philosophical Investigations* and he thought Wittgenstein's letters were of great value not only when they directly referred to his writings but also for providing a sense of Wittgenstein's distinct personality. This historical sensibility is inscribed in his later work as Wittgenstein's literary executor, his editions of Wittgenstein's correspondence and other historical materials, his historical reconstructions of Wittgenstein's two main works and, not least, his increasing awareness of Wittgenstein's *Nachlass* as a literary corpus.[101] All this would lead him to advocate editorial decisions that were quite different from those of Anscombe and Rhees.

Rhees's editing was marked by the highlighting of historical contexts in yet a third sense: he fully immersed himself in studying the internal history of Wittgenstein's thinking and writing, that is, how the writings in his *Nachlass* developed and hung together. His resulting unmatched understanding of the internal relations in Wittgenstein's writings provided the basis for publications that were meant to present readers with missing links in the succession from the *Tractatus* to the *Philosophical Investigations*. Rhees aspired to show this history of Wittgenstein's thought in the way he believed Wittgenstein would have wanted – without scholarly distraction. This idea – of doing what Wittgenstein would have wanted – was like a loadstar for him in his text-immanent historical study of Wittgenstein's writings. In trying to find out what Wittgenstein might have wanted, Rhees built on what he had learned from fifteen years of dialogue with his teacher and friend.

3 The 'Middle Wittgenstein'

3.1 Wittgenstein and Rhees

Of the three literary executors, Rhees knew Wittgenstein the longest. He attended Wittgenstein's lectures for the first time in 1933 and remained his

---

[98] CPE 1967, xiii.   [99] Anscombe, *Wittgenstein's Tractatus*, p. 17.

[100] Wright, *Mitt Liv*, p. 64; Wright, 'Autobiography', 8.

[101] CCO 1973; CRK 1974; PT 1971, 1–34; Wright, 'Origin and Composition', 138–60; Wright, *Wittgenstein*, pp. 63–136.

close and faithful friend until the end of Wittgenstein's life.[102] In contrast to other friends who Wittgenstein advised to leave philosophy, he encouraged Rhees to continue this vocation at the University of Swansea.[103] This may have been partly due to Rhees's constant keenness to develop his own original thinking.

As a youth, Rhees had been expelled from an ethics course at the University of Rochester (where his father was president) on account of his radical views.[104] This led to his leaving the USA and settling in Europe. His first move was to Edinburgh, where he graduated with high honours in 1928, at the age of twenty-three.[105] He then lectured at Manchester and spent long periods in Innsbruck studying the philosophy of Franz Brentano with Alfred Kastil, who was Brentano's literary executor and editor.[106] It was only after this intense work on elaborating Brentano's theory of the continuum that he applied to Cambridge to do doctoral studies. G. E. Moore became his supervisor and advised him to attend Wittgenstein's classes.[107]

Wittgenstein's classes in 1933 had initially put Rhees off. He granted that Wittgenstein's concatenations of similes might be congruent with a philosophical position put forward, but he thought they led to a confusing style of lecturing.[108] Two years later, however, Rhees once again began attending Wittgenstein's classes and found himself increasingly fascinated with Wittgenstein's philosophy. By 1937, he had become a valued discussion partner for Wittgenstein and privy to his plans for publishing. Wittgenstein then asked Rhees to translate his book, which was to be published bilingually by Cambridge University Press under the title *Philosophische Bemerkungen – Philosophical Remarks*.[109] This plan never materialized, partly because Wittgenstein found Rhees's translation 'pretty awful'.[110] This did not, however, affect his opinion that Rhees was 'an excellent man'.[111]

During World War II, Wittgenstein repeatedly visited Rhees in Swansea. These visits enabled Rhees to witness at first hand Wittgenstein's method of philosophical writing.[112] The two discussed and read together Wittgenstein's newly created remarks and Rhees could not help but think that 'his stuff was wonderful'.[113] These visits were most inspiring for Wittgenstein as well. It was

[102] Erbacher, 'Literary Executors', 1–8, 14–17.   [103] WC 2012, 399.

[104] 'Radicalism of Rochester President's Son', *New York Times*, 28 February 1924, 1.

[105] Phillips, 'Biographical Sketch', 267–8.   [106] Erbacher and Schirmer, 'On Continuity', 4–5.

[107] Kastil, 'Nachlass', 5 November 1933, published in Erbacher and Schirmer, 'On Continuity', 6.

[108] Ibid.

[109] PU 2001, 19–21, 205–446; Rhees's translation with notes in Wittgenstein's hand: Ts 226. See Sections 1.4 and A.6 in the present Element.

[110] WC 2012, 292.   [111] Ibid; see also WC 2012, 290 and Erbacher, 'Literary Executors', 8.

[112] Rhees's notes from discussions with Wittgenstein are edited in LA 1966 and more recently in Wittgenstein, Rhees and Citron, 'Conversations with Rush Rhees', 1–71.

[113] Wright, 'Correspondence with Rhees', 27 February 1969, published in Erbacher, 'Literary Executors', 16.

while visiting Rhees in Swansea in 1944 that Wittgenstein stopped elaborating his remarks on the foundations of mathematics and turned to the investigation of psychological concepts.[114] After the war, Wittgenstein resigned from his chair and moved to Ireland to focus on finishing his book.[115] By this time, he had already appointed Rhees as the executor of his will and they continued talking about editing his writings until ten days before Wittgenstein's death.[116]

3.2 'Preliminary Studies'

Rhees was very aware that Wittgenstein had a horror of being misunderstood and misrepresented by eager scholars.[117] As his good friend, literary executor and the executor of his will, Rhees felt duty bound to prevent such misunderstandings. This was one main motive for Rhees's editorial work as a whole and one reason why he began editing two dictations by Wittgenstein, the so-called *Blue and Brown Books*, as soon as the *Remarks on the Foundations of Mathematics* were published in 1956.[118]

The names of the *Blue* and *Brown Books* relate to the coloured cloth bindings of the blank books in which the dictations were originally recorded between 1933 and 1935.[119] Since these dictations were intended to serve didactic purposes and contained Wittgenstein's own English, they were very popular among young scholars who had copied and circulated them privately during Wittgenstein's lifetime and even more so after his death. Rhees was determined to stop this underground trade, not least because he wanted to challenge the view that the language games in the *Blue and Brown Books* constituted a model for Wittgenstein's new philosophical method. Since Rhees regarded this as a misunderstanding, he immediately took measures to publish an authorized edition.

In the introduction, Rhees stressed that the *Blue Book* was nothing more than a set of notes for students who attended Wittgenstein's class in 1933–4, and the *Brown Book* was only a further elaboration of Wittgenstein's ideas from 1935.[120] To make doubly sure that this subordinate status of the texts would not be overlooked (in comparison to the unique status of the *Philosophical Investigations* that Wittgenstein left almost ready for print at the time of his

---

[114] PU 2001, 27–33.

[115] Wright, 'Correspondence with Anscombe', 12 October 1947, published in Erbacher, 'Literary Executors', 23–4.

[116] WC 2012, 395; Wright, 'Correspondence with Rhees', 7 July 1965, published in Erbacher, 'Approaches', 188; Rhees, 'Correspondence with Kenny', 2 March 1977, published in Erbacher, 'Philosophical Reasons', 111.

[117] Cf. CEM 1933; Malcolm, *Memoir*, pp. 56–60.

[118] Mss 309, 310 edited in BBB 1958. See Sections 3.5 and A.4 in the present Element.

[119] See BBB 1958, vii.   [120] BBB 1958, vi–xvi.

death), he gave his publication the subtitle *Preliminary Studies for the 'Philosophical Investigations'*.[121] It is uncertain whether this actually impeded scholars from reading something into the dictations that was not in them. But the subtitle itself may become a source of teleological misunderstanding, inasmuch as it can be understood as presenting texts that were a preparation for something that did not yet exist.

What is in any case clear is that the *Blue* and *Brown Books* were among the last steps in a long development of Wittgenstein's writing that eventually led to the first version of the *Philosophical Investigations*. In fact, the very first version of the *Philosophical Investigations* came into being when Wittgenstein abandoned the idea to translate and revise the *Brown Book* for publication. Working in splendid isolation at his cabin in Skjolden, Norway, in the autumn of 1936, he came to the conclusion that this whole attempt would be 'worthless' and he stopped reworking it.[122] Shortly afterwards, he began writing what is now regarded as the very first version of the *Philosophical Investigations*.[123]

Rhees considered it his duty to make such developments in Wittgenstein's work recognizable for readers. For this reason, publishing the *Blue* and *Brown Books* also functioned as a preliminary study for his subsequent editorial endeavours.

3.3 Returning to the Moore Volume

Having witnessed fifteen years of Wittgenstein's philosophical development at first hand, Rhees had a sense of the tremendous amount of work that lay behind the *Philosophical Investigations*. He was therefore disappointed when, to his mind, readers had missed the depth of the book even a decade after its publication.[124] Pondering over the possible reasons for this neglect, he came to believe that readers could not perceive the long philosophical discussions from which the text of the *Philosophical Investigations* had emerged. He conjectured that people would more readily see what the *Philosophical Investigations* are, and more readily hear what Wittgenstein was saying, if they were able to understand the magnitude of the development underpinning the book. This was the impetus for his editorial ambition: to make recognizable the philosophical development between the *Tractatus* and the *Philosophical Investigations*.

---

[121] A brief discussion about the title can be found in Wright, 'Correspondence with Rhees', autumn 1957.

[122] Ms 115, 292. See Sections 3.5 and A.4 in the present Element.

[123] Ms 142, edited in PU 2001, 51–204. See Sections 2.2, 2.4 and 6.4 and A.5 in the present Element.

[124] Wright, 'Correspondence with Rhees', 4 and 5 September 1962, published in Erbacher, Jung and Seibel, 'Logbook', 114–21.

Wittgenstein's development during the time between the *Tractatus* and the *Philosophical Investigations* is often referred to as 'the middle Wittgenstein', thus – as was also Rhees's intention – to thwart the notion of there being two seemingly distinct Wittgensteins, one 'early' and one 'late', with the early represented by the *Tractatus* and the late by the *Philosophical Investigations*.[125] To counter this simplistic notion that had arisen, Rhees wanted to show that '"the later Wittgenstein" is a continuation of the same discussions which we have in the Tractatus'.[126] To show this, Rhees turned again to the Moore volume.

The Moore volume is made up from cuttings and can be seen as the first fruits of Wittgenstein's return to philosophical writing in 1929.[127] As such, it departs from thinking about the *Tractatus* and shows how a new philosophical development was set into motion. Rhees, who loved copying texts, typed out the Moore volume on his typewriter and, while doing so, became more and more absorbed in tracing the development of Wittgenstein's thinking as it could be seen in the metamorphoses of his manuscripts and typescripts.[128] He searched Wittgenstein's notebooks for handwritten sources of the typewritten remarks in the Moore volume and, in this way, reverse-engineered Wittgenstein's writing practice, as it were.

Rhees thus gradually recognized the movements in Wittgenstein's working process and how they materialized in the literary corpus. Intrigued by this hermeneutic adventure, Rhees asked for a leave of absence from his post as lecturer at the University of Swansea in 1963, in order to concentrate fully on Wittgenstein's papers.[129]

3.4 Philosophical Discussions

While typing out the Moore volume, Rhees recognized that the philosophical view put forward could greatly clarify Wittgenstein's relation to the Vienna Circle:

> It was a view which was very influencial [sic] at the time, although it was not understood. It influenced Schlick, and I think it influenced Carnap; and perhaps some others. People are *still* unclear about the influence of Wittgenstein on the Wiener Kreis [Vienna Circle], and they try to ascribe

---

[125] Cf. Stern, 'How many Wittgensteins?', 164–88.

[126] Wright, 'Correspondence with Rhees', 10 February 1962, published in Erbacher, Jung and Seibel, 'Logbook', 125.

[127] Ts 209, edited in PB 1964. See Sections 2.1, 2.3, 3.4, 3.5, 4.2 and 4.5 and A.2 in the present Element.

[128] Erbacher, 'Philosophical Reasons', 121–3.

[129] Wright, 'Correspondence with Rhees', 10 February 1963, published in Erbacher, Jung and Seibel, 'Logbook', 122.

this influence to the Tractatus. This generally leads them to read the Tractatus wrongly. I think the MM [Moore Volume] is interesting because it shows both the source of the impetus of much of the early work of the logical positivists, and also how hopeless it was to look for a clue to Wittgenstein's views in their misunderstandings of him.[130]

By typing out the remarks into a continuous typescript, Rhees discovered the vagaries of Wittgenstein's punctuation and wondered what to make of them in the printed edition.[131] But soon he remembered that Wittgenstein 'wrote "by ear" more than "by eye"', and thus the punctuation is a helpful score for reading aloud, which reveals more readily the rhythm and meaning of his remarks.[132] This observation chimed with Wittgenstein's need for discussion partners who spurred his thinking.[133] It was therefore not a complete surprise – although, at the same time, it was unexpected and most welcome news – that the papers of the late Friedrich Waismann in Oxford contained notes of discussions with Wittgenstein and even dictations that stemmed from the same period as the Moore volume.[134]

Wittgenstein, Waismann and Moritz Schlick had met several times in Vienna in 1929–30 and Waismann had even cooperated with Wittgenstein to create a systematic presentation of the latter's philosophical views.[135] Following Wittgenstein, Waismann had immigrated to Cambridge in the mid-1930s, but when Wittgenstein broke off contact with him he moved to Oxford.[136] In 1959 Waismann died. Like Wittgenstein, he had appointed three literary executors who, in turn, had appointed Brian McGuinness to work on the papers.[137]

McGuinness had already come to the attention of Wittgenstein's literary executors due to his work on the new translation of the *Tractatus*, done in collaboration with David Pears.[138] He was now preparing a publication of the notes Waismann made from discussions with Wittgenstein. McGuinness and Rhees entered into an exchange about the materials that stemmed from the same period and Rhees even included some drafts taken from Waismann's

---

[130] Wright, 'Correspondence with Rhees', 10 February 1963, published in Erbacher, Jung and Seibel, 'Logbook', 123; cf. Rhees, 'Seeds of Some Misunderstandings', 213–20.

[131] Wright, 'Correspondence with Rhees', 12 August 1962, published in Erbacher, Jung and Seibel, 'Logbook', 113–14.

[132] Wright, 'Correspondence with Rhees', 14 February 1963, published in Erbacher, Jung and Seibel, 'Logbook', 126.

[133] In a talk near Siena in 2018, McGuinness emphasized that this aspect would be a rich topic for future research.

[134] Schulte, 'Waismann-Nachlass', 108–40.   [135] WWK 1967, WLP 1965, 1976, VW 2003.

[136] McGuinness, *Approaches*, pp. 177–200; McGuinness, 'Irrfahrten', 41–53.

[137] Waismann's literary executors were Stuart Hampshire, Isaiah Berlin and Gilbert Ryle.

[138] TLP 1961.

papers as appendices in his edition of the Moore volume.[139] This was published under the title *Philosophische Bemerkungen* (*Philosophical Remarks*) in 1964.[140]

To help readers of the *Philosophical Remarks* recognize what Rhees took as Wittgenstein's philosophical orientation – an orientation that was incompatible with a scientific worldview as championed by the Vienna Circle – he included a draft for a preface from 1930. In this draft, Wittgenstein stated that his book was written in a spirit that is 'different from the one which informs the vast stream of European and American civilization in which all of us stand'.[141] With this editorial framing of *Philosophische Bemerkungen*, Rhees clearly influenced how the book would be read and this is precisely what he wanted to achieve. He wanted to make readers see 'the ways Wittgenstein went, and he tried to make readers see the material with Wittgenstein's eyes'.[142]

3.5 Discovering the *Philosophical Grammar*

Although Rhees's next editorial project – *Philosophische Grammatik* (*Philosophical Grammar*)[143] – appeared five years after *Philosophical Remarks*, these books are two aspects of one editorial aim: to elucidate the path from the *Tractatus* to the *Philosophical Investigations*. *Philosophical Remarks* is the first steppingstone in this trajectory and *Philosophical Grammar* is the second.

Editing *Philosophical Grammar* began with a unique item among Wittgenstein's papers: the so-called 'Big Typescript', which is a 768-page collection of remarks, divided into nineteen sections and 140 chapters.[144] The literary executors had been intrigued by this monumental document for a long time, but had postponed editing it.[145] In the early 1960s, Rhees finally took the Big Typescript off the shelf and read it at the same time as he typed out the Moore volume.[146] He thereby realized that a huge philosophical development had taken place during the three or four years between the scripts: while the search for definite building blocks of language still animated the Moore volume (stemming from 1930), the Big Typescript (stemming from 1933–4)

---

[139] Rhees, 'Correspondence with McGuinness', 1962–4. McGuinness's papers may be studied soon in the Forschungsinstitut Brenner Archive at the University of Innsbruck.

[140] PB 1964.

[141] PB 1975, foreword. The entire draft of the preface can be found in Ms 109, 204–8.

[142] Wolfgang Kienzler suggested this phrasing in a review of the manuscript for the present Element.

[143] PG 1969, first English version PG 1974. I refer to the work by its English name for sake of ease.

[144] Ts 213, edited in Will and BT 2005. See Sections 2.4 and 5.1 and A.3 in the present Element.

[145] Wright, 'Correspondence with Rhees', 2 March 1952, published in Erbacher, 'Approaches', 173.

[146] Erbacher, Jung and Seibel, 'Logbook', 105–47.

had given up the picture of meaning as being fixed.[147] Instead, Wittgenstein now investigated a word's meaning through understanding its role in the context in which it was used. His investigation had thus changed from an analysis of fixed meaning to a 'grammatical' investigation.[148] From here, there was just one more step to the language games of the *Blue* and *Brown Books*. In fact, the concept of 'language game' was already present in the Big Typescript.[149] Naturally then, the Big Typescript was the prime candidate for closing the gap that still yawned between the *Philosophical Remarks* and the *Blue* and *Brown Books*.

Its well-structured first appearance notwithstanding, editing the Big Typescript became a very complex endeavour, for Rhees's copy of it was full of Wittgenstein's corrections.[150] Rhees therefore suspected that Wittgenstein had not thought of the Big Typescript as a book in its own right, but rather as a well-sorted storehouse of remarks to be used for writing a new book.[151] Rhees's conjecture was confirmed when another large manuscript surfaced; it contained the very same text that emerged when Rhees carried out Wittgenstein's handwritten corrections to the Big Typescript.[152] It was this 'Revision', as Wittgenstein had called it, that Rhees regarded as a 'continuous book' by Wittgenstein.[153] Wittgenstein had entitled the whole ledger 'Philosophical Grammar' – and that was the title Rhees used for the book that he published: 'If I can produce a book at all, I think it should be called *Philosophische Grammatik*.'[154]

However, while following the traces in the Revision, Rhees came across yet another manuscript of the same text that contained even more revisions by Wittgenstein.[155] The editorial ambition to publish *Philosophical Grammar* amounted, therefore, to a task that Rhees described thus:

> What I hoped would be the chief work in this period – what I had hoped was a manuscript with corrections and variants which need to be edited – has now

---

[147] Wright, 'Correspondence with Rhees', 14 January 1964, published in Erbacher, Jung and Seibel, 'Logbook', 129–40.
[148] Wright, 'Correspondence with Rhees', 10 February 1963, published in Erbacher, Jung and Seibel, 'Logbook', 124.
[149] See A.3 in the present Element, e.g. Ts 213, 79r. For the development of the concept of grammar between the Big Typescript and the *Blue* and *Brown Books*, see Uffelmann, *Vom System zum Gebrauch*, pp. 103–81.
[150] Rhees's copy is part of the 'Rhees Papers' kept at the Wren Library at Trinity College Cambridge.
[151] Erbacher, 'Philosophical Reasons', 127–30.
[152] Ms 114, 31v–45r and Ms 115, 1–117. See Sections 3.6 and 5.1 and A.3 in the present Element.
[153] Wright, 'Correspondence with Rhees', 8 November 1965, published in Erbacher, 'Philosophical Reasons', 127.
[154] Wright, 'Correspondence with Rhees', 8 November 1965, published in Erbacher, 'Philosophical Reasons', 128.
[155] Ms 140. See Sections 3.6 and 5.1 and A.3 in the present Element.

turned out to be not Siamese twins but Siamese quadruplets. And I wish I would see how to make it plain what this quartet is saying.[156]

3.6 The High Point of Rhees's Co-Creational Editing

After *Philosophical Remarks* was published in 1964, Rhees resigned from his post at the University of Swansea and fully immersed himself in Wittgenstein's papers. Thousands of pages in the Rhees Archives show that, for him, editing Wittgenstein was not external to the development of his own philosophical understanding.[157] On the contrary, for almost every calendar day, there are sheets filled with both philosophical and exegetical notes that evolved simultaneously to his editorial work. They testify that Rhees scrutinized how changes in Wittgenstein's philosophical discussions went hand-in-hand with changes in the arrangement of his remarks. In this context, he remembered watching Wittgenstein make changes:

> [He] cut out certain things (sometimes to my bewilderment) and change[d] the order or passages; having seen him change one version for another (this was with the earlier versions of the Philosophische Untersuchungen), and [I] heard him treat the same materials in his lectures; remembering especially the reasons he often did give for cutting out, revising and shortening what he said was 'foul'; so that I could see something of the same way of working and the same standards in some of the crossings out and revisions in manuscripts.[158]

By repeating the changes through his practice of typing, Rhees relived the metamorphoses of Wittgenstein's writings and became aware of how differing arrangements of the same or similar remarks could generate very different philosophical discussions.[159] This editorial re-enactment of Wittgenstein's philosophical discussions, as documented in Wittgenstein's writings, became Rhees's philosophical discussions with both himself and Wittgenstein and with Wittgenstein's having philosophical discussions with himself.

After more than three years, Rhees's simultaneously editorial, hermeneutical, philosophical and literary adventure resulted in one single typewritten text, the one Rhees published under the title *Philosophical Grammar* in 1969.[160] This

---

[156] Rhees, 'Correspondence with Drury', 7 November 1965, published in Erbacher, 'Approaches', 183.

[157] The Rush Rhees Collection, which is said to contain 160,000 pages in manuscript form (Phillips, 'Biographical Sketch', 275), is kept at the Richard Burton Archives at the University of Swansea.

[158] Rhees, 'Correspondence with Kenny', 2 March 1977, published in Erbacher, 'Philosophical Reasons', 117.

[159] Wright, 'Correspondence Rhees', 14 January 1964, published in Erbacher, 'Philosophical Reasons', 125–6.

[160] PG 1969, first English version PG 1974.

book is the result of a philosophical co-creation: just as Wittgenstein had described the aim of his philosophizing as a search to find 'intermediate cases', Rhees, with the *Philosophical Grammar*, created an intermediate case in the morphology of Wittgenstein's development as a philosophical writer.[161] To make this visible, Rhees originally wanted to divide the *Philosophical Grammar* into two volumes – a feature that would characterize the further development into the *Philosophical Investigations*. The publisher, however, refused to divide the book in this way.[162] But this decision was certainly not the only reason why the book was not received in the way that Rhees may have hoped. The apocryphal work would become a main target for textual criticism, once scholars gained access to copies of Wittgenstein's papers.

4 The Wittgenstein Papers

4.1 Wittgenstein's Last Writings

Neither Anscombe nor von Wright had a familiarity with Wittgenstein's *Nachlass* that compared to that of Rhees. This became obvious when Anscombe and von Wright edited Wittgenstein's writings from the last two years of his life.[163] At that time, Wittgenstein had already been informed that he was incurably ill, and he had stopped elaborating the remarks that were to be included in the *Philosophical Investigations*.[164] But this did not stop him from thinking and writing altogether. In fact, he wrote philosophical remarks until he lost consciousness two days before he died.

The set of manuscripts that Wittgenstein wrote during the last months of his life, and which were not supposed to become part of the *Philosophical Investigations*, formed a certain sub-corpus in the *Nachlass* that the literary executors called the 'Omega volumes'.[165] Anscombe and von Wright used them to edit *On Certainty, Remarks on Colour* and *Last Writings on the Philosophy of Psychology II*.[166]

Anscombe and von Wright's draft for the preface of the most popular of these books – *On Certainty* – stated that Malcolm had triggered these investigations in mid-1949. Rhees objected vehemently: maybe the discussions with Malcolm had stimulated Wittgenstein to take up these thoughts and to develop them

---

[161] cf. PI §122 and Erbacher, 'Philosophical Reasons', 127–130.

[162] The title for the first volume was to be 'Satz, Sinn des Satzes' and the second 'Über Logik und Mathematik', the latter not being a part of Wittgenstein's 'Revision'. The correspondence between Rhees and the publisher can be found in the Rush Rhees Collection at the Richard Burton Archives.

[163] Mss 169–77; cf. Schulte, 'Last Writings', 63–78. See Sections 5.5 and A.10 in the present Element.

[164] PU 2001, 12–50.   [165] Wright, 'Correspondence with Rhees', 29 January 1962.

[166] OC 1969, ROC 1977, LW 1992.

further, but it would be misleading not to recognize the constant connections between these remarks and the earlier discussions in his oeuvre that dated back at least to 1930.[167] Hence, Rhees proposed printing the remarks gathered in *On Certainty* together with Wittgenstein's *Lecture on Ethics* and *Remarks on Frazer's Golden Bough*, because he believed it was important to highlight the connection between *On Certainty* and Wittgenstein's earlier thinking on the limits of science.[168] Anscombe rejected this idea, as she believed these earlier writings would be 'tacked on' to Wittgenstein's last writings.[169] In contrast to Rhees's holistic view of Wittgenstein's oeuvre, she and von Wright decided to arrange the remarks from the Omega volumes in several books under titles that could more easily relate to specializations in analytical philosophy, for instance epistemology (*On Certainty*) and philosophies of perception or psychology (*Remarks on Colour*, *Last Writings on the Philosophy of Psychology*). Of course, this was certainly different from the reading that Rhees would have wanted to inspire in a publication of Wittgenstein's last writings.

Despite the literary executors' great differences in reading Wittgenstein, the publications made by Anscombe and von Wright show a striking similarity to those made by Rhees: all three editors believed it was right to create books without heavy annotation or learned commentary and that their philosophical understanding of the texts should inform their editorial decisions. This was the common ground in their interpretation of Wittgenstein's will, even though they read his writings differently.

A further edited volume by Anscombe and von Wright shows their 'philosophical editing' paradigmatically: the volume *Zettel*.[170] *Zettel* (German for 'cuttings') contains mostly remarks from the period between 1945 and 1948, that is, after Wittgenstein finished working on the typescript used for *Philosophical Investigations* Part I, yet before he composed the material used for *Philosophical Investigations* Part II (1949). *Zettel* thus represents a branch of Wittgenstein's work that grew during the post-war years, mainly during his last two years as a philosophy professor at Cambridge. This was a time when his work had already shifted towards investigating psychological concepts. As the title of Anscombe and von Wright's edited volume suggests, the book is made from a collection of cuttings. Wittgenstein reworked these and had partly bundled them into groups. It was in this arrangement that the literary executors

---

[167] Wright, 'Correspondence with Rhees', 18 June 1969, edited in Rhees, 'New Topic?', 3–5. Because of this letter, von Wright asked Rhees to write a preface to OC, but this preface was only posthumously published in Rhees, 'Preface', 61–6.

[168] LE 1965, GB 1967, GB 1971; Rhees and von Wright's discussion about OC is to be found in Wright, 'Correspondence with Rhees', June 1969–March 1970.

[169] Wright, 'Correspondence with Rhees', 19 March 1970.   [170] Z 1967.

received them. But the sequence of the remarks in the printed volume does not represent Wittgenstein's exact arrangement of them: although Wittgenstein's cut-and-paste material is said to have remained together, Anscombe's husband, Peter Geach, wove the ungrouped remarks into the places where he himself thought they fit best.[171] However, readers of the volume are not told which remarks were grouped by Wittgenstein and which by Geach. At the time of the editing, it did not occur to the editors that this information would be relevant; what they had in mind, rather, was to present, in the most easily accessible way, what they regarded as Wittgenstein's philosophical work from a certain period or on a certain topic.

An alternative to this 'philosophical editing' in the first two decades after Wittgenstein's death would evolve only as a consequence of von Wright's subsequent work as Wittgenstein's literary heir, through new projects that paved the way for a more historically informed type of editing.

4.2 Copies to Cornell?

Until the mid-1960s, the literary executors' handling of the material documents of Wittgenstein's writings might have driven professional historians and librarians to despair. Rhees and Anscombe kept the manuscripts and typescripts at their homes, working with them, sometimes writing notes in them and exposing them to the dangers of daily life – sometimes with disastrous consequences: the typescripts from which PI 1953 was typeset were lost; Anscombe is said to have burnt a section that referred to a then-living person; Rhees's dog tried to eat one of the manuscripts; and Rhees himself lost the original of the Moore volume in a telephone booth at Paddington Station in London.[172] Furthermore, since there was little collaboration with scholars outside the triumvirate of literary heirs, very few people had seen the originals from which the three heirs were crafting publications. Now, as more and more posthumous books were published, scholars became interested in seeing the actual documents from which the books were made. One such scholar was Norman Malcolm.

Von Wright had kept Malcolm updated about the literary executors' discoveries and decisions.[173] Malcolm, just like Rhees and von Wright, was fascinated to discover for himself the 'middle Wittgenstein', all the more so because he was drafting an encyclopaedia article about Wittgenstein's life work.[174] During Anscombe's research stay in Ithaca in 1963, Malcolm asked her whether it would be possible for Cornell to be a depository for copies of the manuscripts

---

[171] cf. Erbacher, 'Approaches', 185–6.

[172] Cf. Paul, *Progress*, p. 13; Wright, *Mitt Liv*, p. 159; Rhees, 'Letter to von Wright', 26 July 1962, published in Erbacher, Jung and Seibel, 'Logbook', 111–13).

[173] Wright, 'Correspondence with Malcolm', 1947–90.   [174] Malcolm, 'Wittgenstein', 327–40.

from Wittgenstein's middle period.[175] Anscombe favoured the idea and so did von Wright – but Rhees bitterly vetoed any copying.[176] He trusted Malcolm just as much as Anscombe and von Wright did, but he remembered when Malcolm's notes from lectures had been copied and circulated without Malcolm or the literary executors being aware of it. Rhees feared the same thing would happen once there were copies of Wittgenstein's manuscripts – and he was sure that this was the last thing Wittgenstein would have wanted.

Rhees feared that scholars would try to use Wittgenstein's manuscripts as a quarry, digging in them to find support for their own idiosyncratic readings – or to try to reveal scandals – without caring to understand the status of the manuscripts in the body of Wittgenstein's work as a whole.[177] Rhees had seen this done with the published parts of the pre-Tractarian writings and he antici-pated the same misuse if other manuscripts were in circulation. Von Wright eventually agreed with Rhees and especially so when it came to Wittgenstein's coded entries.[178] The literary executors had seen Wittgenstein's code in the pre-Tractarian notebooks and regarded them as purely private notes.[179] Passages in the same coded form were scattered throughout the *Nachlass*,[180] but no one at that time knew exactly how many coded remarks there were or what they said. With Malcolm's request for copies, it became clear to the literary executors that they ought to gain an overview of all such coded material.

Von Wright therefore informed Malcolm that the literary executors had decided to decipher all the coded remarks before deciding whether or not to make a copy of Wittgenstein's *Nachlass*.[181] Von Wright then systematically searched all the papers in his possession for coded remarks. This was the beginning of his historical systematization of all of Wittgenstein's papers.

4.3 Beautiful and Deep Remarks

While decoding the coded remarks, von Wright also searched the *Nachlass* for aphorisms on broad topics such as religion, culture, life or work in philosophy. As he collected these remarks, he was struck by their 'beauty and depth'.[182] He remembered that he had had a similar feeling ten years earlier while editing the

---

[175] Wright, 'Correspondence with Malcolm', 6 June 1963.
[176] Wright. 'Correspondence with Rhees', 7 July 1965, published in Erbacher, 'Omitted Stuff', 91–2.
[177] Wright. 'Correspondence with Rhees', 17 December 1966, published in Erbacher, 'Omitted Stuff', 93.
[178] Ibid.   [179] See Sections 2.1, 2.5, 4.3, 4.5, 5.4 and 5.6 and A.1 in the present Element.
[180] A diary (Ms 183) with long passages in code has been edited in DB 1997a, DB 1997b and DB 2003, 3–255; Somavilla, 'Coded Remarks', 30–50.
[181] Wright, 'Correspondence with Malcolm', 13 October 1965.
[182] Wright, 'Correspondence with Rhees', 13 December 1974, published in Erbacher, 'Omitted Stuff', 100.

Remarks on the Foundations of Mathematics. Some of the remarks they had omitted from that publication had impressed von Wright so much that he had already begun toying with the idea of publishing a collection of beautiful aphorisms.[183] Von Wright thus compiled a selection that could comprise a volume of 'general remarks', as he now called them.[184]

By 1965 an assemblage of more than 1,500 'general remarks' from about sixty manuscripts and typescripts was ready.[185] Von Wright thought this was a fascinating collection for the literary executors, but he did not think the compilation was publishable.[186] In particular, he thought the general remarks were far too 'detached' from Wittgenstein's philosophy to be justifiably published, as he stated in a note appended to his selection.[187] This opinion shifted, however, when von Wright underwent a change concerning the question of what philosophy ought to be. Mainly due to the USA's Vietnam War policy, he was increasingly concerned with social and political questions and became convinced that the treatment of such questions could be a justified part of a philosopher's work.[188] In light of this reorientation regarding what philosophy can be, von Wright reread his selection of Wittgenstein's general remarks. These now appeared to have new significance for understanding Wittgenstein's philosophy: rather than being mere by-products of Wittgenstein's philosophical remarks, the general remarks made it possible to read what Wittgenstein thought about life and culture and his work therein.

The general remarks offered von Wright a frame for understanding Wittgenstein's philosophical work as a whole.[189] Rhees had ascribed a similar function to *Wittgenstein's Lecture on Ethics* and his *Remarks on Frazer's Golden Bough*.[190] All of these writings can provide a clue to Wittgenstein's philosophical orientation, the understanding of which both Rhees and von Wright considered paramount to understanding his philosophical work. Since von Wright recognized that the learned world still saw Wittgenstein as a 'cultural illiterate', he thought the publication of the general remarks would be justified as an antidote.[191] Indeed,

---

[183] Wright, 'Correspondence with Anscombe', 6 November 1954, published in Erbacher, 'Omitted Stuff', 88.
[184] The unpublished collection of "General Remarks" was compiled in spring 1965, cf. Erbacher, 'Omitted Stuff', 89–91.
[185] Cf. Rothhaupt, 'General Remarks', 103–36.
[186] Wright, 'Correspondence with Anscombe', 20 June 1965.
[187] Wright, 'Note', published in Erbacher, 'Omitted Stuff', 90.
[188] Österman, 'Healing the Rift', 1–18; Erbacher, 'Omitted Stuff', 94–9.
[189] VB 1977, preface; Wright, 'His times', 201–16.
[190] LE 1965, GB 1967, GB 1971; Wright, 'Correspondence with Rhees', 5 March 1970. For an account of Rhees's editing of the Remarks on Frazer, see Westergaard, 'Ketner and Eigsti edition', 117–42.
[191] Wright, *Wittgenstein*, p. 3.

when he eventually presented *Vermischte Bemerkungen* in his keynote lecture at the second Wittgenstein Symposium at Kirchberg in 1977, it was the dawn of a hitherto unknown and culturally subversive Wittgenstein that hit a younger generation of scholars like a 'bombshell'.[192]

4.4 Wittgenstein and von Wright

Von Wright's sensitivity for Wittgenstein's general remarks may be better understood when taking into account the history of the two men's acquaintance. Von Wright came to Cambridge for a study period abroad as a PhD student in 1939.[193] At that time, he was a convinced logical positivist. His mentor in Helsinki, Eino Kaila, had been collaborating with the Vienna Circle and taught von Wright to read the *Tractatus* as the agenda for a scientific philosophy to be spelled out by a future generation of professionals.[194] Naturally, von Wright had wanted to go to Vienna for his research stay abroad, but since the Vienna Circle had been dissolved, Cambridge was the next best choice and the best place to deepen his work on inductive logic.[195] When he arrived at Cambridge, he was surprised to learn that Wittgenstein was teaching there. Von Wright attended Wittgenstein's lectures and immediately felt he was witnessing intellectual events of historic significance. Still, his personal discussions with Wittgenstein made an even bigger impression on him.[196]

Von Wright recognized that Wittgenstein was the philosophical genius that he had expected – but, to his great surprise, he also encountered Wittgenstein as a representative of a great German-Austrian high culture.[197] This culture was part of his own paternal heritage and he still admired it, even while it was on the verge of disappearing.[198] An embodiment of this 'world of yesterday' remained a central aspect of von Wright's picture of Wittgenstein, also when von Wright returned to Cambridge after World War II – first to attend Wittgenstein's very last lectures in 1947 and then to succeed him as a professor of philosophy in 1948.[199] During the subsequent period, Wittgenstein sometimes lived at von Wright's house:

> When Wittgenstein was with us, he and I had daily talks, sometimes on things
> he was working on then, sometimes on the logical topics which were mine at

---

[192] VB 1977; Janik, 'Remembering Kirchberg 1977', 94–5.   [193] Wright, *Mitt Liv*, pp. 71–8.

[194] Wright, 'Logistik filosofi', 175–7; Wright, '*Mitt Liv*', pp. 54–8; Wright, 'Autobiography', 5.

[195] Wright, *Mitt Liv*, pp. 68–70, cf. Wright, *Wahrscheinlichkeit*; Broad, 'Hr. von Wright', 1–24, 97–119, 193–214.

[196] Erbacher, 'Literary Executors', 11–13.

[197] cf. Toulmin and Janik, *Vienna*, and Janik, *Revisited*.

[198] Wright, 'Correspondence with Kaila', 6 June 1939; cf. Österman, 'Perfect Viennese', and Toulmin and Janik, *Vienna*, p. 11.

[199] Wright, *Mitt Liv*, pp. 132–3; Erbacher, 'Literary Executors', 21–5.

the time, but most often on literature and music, on religion, and on what could perhaps best be termed the philosophy of history and civilization. Wittgenstein sometimes read to me from his favourite authors, for example, from Grimm's Maerchen [Fairy Tales] or Gottfried Keller's Zuericher Novellen. The recollection of his voice and facial expression when, seated in a chair in his sickroom, he read aloud Goethe's Hermann und Dorothea is for me unforgettable.[200]

This is the background that prepared von Wright to appreciate Wittgenstein's greatness as a philosopher who 'ranked among the classic writers of German prose'.[201] Von Wright's resulting ambition – to provide access to texts and documents that would allow readers to see Wittgenstein as a man embedded in his historical, social and cultural context – is a clue to unify the different aspects of his work as Wittgenstein's literary heir: he published books from Wittgenstein's *Nachlass*, preserved and made available the whole corpus of Wittgenstein's writings and correspondence and produced studies on the origins of Wittgenstein's works.

4.5 Preserving Wittgenstein's *Nachlass*

When von Wright compiled the first collection of general remarks in 1965, he realized that not even he had a complete set of photocopies of Wittgenstein's writings.[202] He also knew that the documents in Anscombe's and Rhees's homes were constantly in danger; as already stated, the typescripts from which the *Philosophical Investigations* had been printed had already been lost and the same was the case for the Moore volume that Rhees had left behind in a telephone booth.[203] Von Wright therefore wanted to take measures to preserve all the papers for future research. He revived the idea that Malcom had already aired, of creating a copy of some of the manuscripts, but now expanded it to include the entire *Nachlass*.[204] Rhees still disliked the idea and it would take serious negotiations to convince him.[205] However, when the *Philosophische Grammatik* was about to be published, he saw less reason for vetoing the idea. Since Malcolm had negotiated with Cornell University to cover the expenses for

---

[200] Wright, 'Autobiography', 15.

[201] Wright, 'Biographical Sketch', 544; Anscombe held a similar view, cf. Erbacher, dos Santos Reis and Jung, 'BBC radio talk', 239.

[202] Wright, 'Correspondence with Malcolm', 3 December 1966. Von Wright estimated that there were 1,000 pages in Oxford and 1,500 pages in Swansea of which he had no photocopies.

[203] See Section 4.2 in the present Element. Later, parts of the *Nachlass* kept in Austria were auctioned at Sotheby & Co; see Wright, 'Correspondence with Rhees', 1969.

[204] Wright, 'Correspondence with Rhees', 15 December 1965, published in Erbacher, 'Omitted Stuff', 93.

[205] Erbacher, 'Omitted Stuff', 91–4.

producing a microfilm and arranged for both himself and von Wright to supervise the filming, Rhees eventually agreed:

> Elizabeth and Rhees have now replied to our new proposal concerning the filming of Wittgenstein's Nachlass. They give their consent – Rhees too, I understand, but his letter was *very* emotional and he *hates* the idea.[206]

Another year passed before von Wright put all the manuscripts in heavy suitcases and took them to Oxford.[207] Thus, together with the material in Anscombe's possession, the greater part of the then-known items in Wittgenstein's *Nachlass* were collected in Oxford and it was there that the microfilming took place between 1967 and 1968.[208] But the literary executors still did not want to make Wittgenstein's coded remarks available. To this end, they first produced an uncensored microfilm, then indicated the passages to be covered up during a second filming.[209] Wittgenstein's remarks in code were therefore still inaccessible to scholars. But apart from this censorship, the microfilm recorded the entirety of the then-known writings of Wittgenstein. The film was sent to Cornell University and there copied onto paper, resulting in 117 bound volumes.

The Cornell University Library also produced a catalogue of the papers, called 'The Wittgenstein Papers'.[210] But as von Wright discovered, there were many mistakes in this catalogue. He went through the film once more and created a comprehensively revised catalogue, using a numbering system that assigned an unambiguous reference to each item and distinguished between manuscripts, typescripts and dictations.[211] The publishing of this catalogue – which still provides the authoritative structure of Wittgenstein's *Nachlass* – together with the announcement that research institutions could purchase copies of Wittgenstein's papers from Cornell University, enabled scholars to access Wittgenstein's *Nachlass*.[212]

After the Cornell microfilm was produced, Rhees and Anscombe gave the papers in their possession to Trinity College Cambridge. These are now in the Wren Library.[213] Thus, after eighteen years of editing, Wittgenstein's writings found a safe home.

---

[206] Wright, 'Correspondence with Malcolm', 3 December 1966. The agreement was signed in the spring of 1967.

[207] Wright, 'Correspondence with Rhees', October 1968.

[208] Wright, 'Wittgenstein Papers', 38.

[209] The idea of covering up the coded remarks was originally Malcolm's; see Erbacher, 'Omitted Stuff', 93.

[210] Wright, 'Correspondence with Rhees', 18 November 1968.

[211] Wright, 'Wittgenstein Papers', 35–62.

[212] For critical discussions of the catalogue structure, see Schmidt, 'Some Suggestions', and Smith, 'Documenting Macroprocess'.

[213] An agreement with Trinity College had been reached, according to which the copyright would be transferred to the college after the death of the last surviving literary executor. It was agreed, however, that they would appoint successors who should, as a board of trustees, continue to

5 First Steps towards a Scholarly Edition

5.1 A Scholarly Attack

The Cornell microfilm and von Wright's catalogue aided all subsequent scholarship on Wittgenstein's *Nachlass*. One of the first scholars outside the circle of literary heirs who inspected the Cornell microfilm was Anthony Kenny, lecturer at Oxford at that time. He had drafted a translation of the *Philosophische Grammatik* into English during a stay at the University of Heidelberg in early summer 1972.[214] In late summer of that same year, he was staying with his father-in-law at Ithaca and accessed the microfilm. Consulting the copy of the Big Typescript, Kenny discovered that the sources for the *Philosophische Grammatik* were much more 'heterogeneous' than he had expected from reading the book.[215] He then suggested writing up an account of the differences and to include it as a translator's note to the English edition, together with the Big Typescript's impressive table of contents.[216]

Given the long philosophical co-creation process for the *Philosophische Grammatik*, it is easy to imagine that Rhees saw no point in Kenny's proposal.[217] Kenny accepted this rejection at first, but eventually published his account of the differences in the essay 'From the Big Typescript to the *Philosophical Grammar*'.[218] Here he argued that although Rhees had spared no efforts to present a definitive revision of the Big Typescript, this ambition was actually unfulfilled and would be impossible to fulfil; it would necessarily involve so many arbitrary decisions that it would be better to publish the original typescript as it stood.[219] Most strikingly, Kenny revealed that both the German and the English versions excluded whole chapters from the middle of the Big Typescript, such as the chapter entitled 'Philosophy', thus also excluding Wittgenstein's 'vivid metaphors for philosophical method'.[220]

---

advise the college when questions arose concerning publications from Wittgenstein's *Nachlass*. After this agreement was reached, Anscombe too moved to Cambridge in 1969, because she was given – after von Wright and John Wisdom – the professorship that once had been held by Wittgenstein.

[214] Rhees, 'Correspondence with Kenny', 27 August 1972.

[215] Ibid. See Sections 2.4 and 3.5 and A.3 in the present Element.   [216] Ibid.

[217] Rhees, 'Correspondence with Kenny', 27 February 1973, published in Erbacher, 'Philosophical Reasons', 137–8. See Sections 3.5 and 3.6 in the present Element.

[218] Kenny, 'To the *Philosophical Grammar*'. Interestingly, Kenny's essay appeared in an honorary volume for von Wright.

[219] Ibid, 41–53.

[220] Ibid, 45; Rhees excluded the chapters 'Philosophy' (Ts 213, 406r-435r), 'Phenomenology' (Ts 213, 436r–485r) and 'Idealism' (Ts 213, 486r–528r) in the Big Typescript (Ts 213) from *Philosophical Grammar*. See Sections 2.4 and 3.5 and A.3 in the present Element.

According to Kenny, any reader must find it strange that 'these important and fascinating chapters' had been silently omitted.[221]

In actual fact, Rhees had neither aspired to present a definitive revision of the Big Typescript nor to keep the 'Philosophy' chapter from the public, but this was the impression one could easily get from reading Kenny's article.[222] It took up and reinforced a suspicion that Kenny described to Rhees thus:

> I think that the general philosophical public feels rather about the Wittgenstein Nachlass as the Roman plebs felt about Caesar's will. There are these triumvirs, and we only have their word for what is in the will. Who knows whether Caesar may not have left us all his gardens on both sides of the Tiber?[223]

Rhees did not care about that; he only asked himself:

> 'What would Wittgenstein have wanted? Would he have wanted it this way? Is this faintly like what he would have done or have wanted us to do?' I think this is more in my thoughts than anything else. NOT: 'What does the general philosophical public want?'[224]

Even so, Kenny's essay showed that a new generation of Wittgenstein scholars with a heightened text-critical awareness was emerging. *From the Big Typescript to the Philosophical Grammar* would become a blueprint for a new kind of Wittgenstein philology and for the scholarly criticism of the literary executors' editorial work.

5.2 Philological Criticism I: Oxford Scholars and von Wright

One centre for new text-critical Wittgenstein scholarship was Oxford. At Balliol College, Kenny gave lectures on the 'middle Wittgenstein' and these were attended by, among others, a young student from Germany, Joachim Schulte.[225] Both Kenny and Schulte would become trustees of Wittgenstein's *Nachlass* many years later.[226] Schulte was also a pupil and later colleague and friend of McGuinness, who was another protagonist of the historically and philologically oriented Wittgenstein scholarship at Oxford. Inspired by Gilbert Ryle's lectures in the 1950s, he and David Pears had created

---

[221] Kenny, 'To the *Philosophical Grammar*', 47.

[222] Wright, 'Correspondence with Rhees', 22 January 1976, published in Erbacher, 'Philosophical Reasons', 135.

[223] Rhees, 'Correspondence with Kenny', 20 March 1973, published in Erbacher, 'Philosophical Reasons', 138.

[224] Rhees, 'Correspondence with Kenny', 22 March 1973, published in Erbacher, 'Philosophical Reasons', 138–9.

[225] Schulte, 'Memories', 187.

[226] See note 214 in Section 4.5 and see Section 6.2 in the present Element.

a *Tractatus* translation that was meant to be closer to Wittgenstein's German than the earlier translation by Frank P. Ramsey.[227] In the 1960s, McGuinness edited the papers of the late Waismann (who was another source of importing Wittgenstein's thought to Oxford) and was in contact with Rhees concerning that.[228] Now McGuinness shared his scholarly orientation with von Wright. They collaborated on editing an early version of the *Tractatus* that von Wright had found in Austria on a visit in 1965, the so-called *Prototractatus*, producing a bibliophile facsimile edition enriched with von Wright's study of the origins of the *Tractatus*.[229]

With a similar historical and text-critical interest, von Wright then turned to the *Philosophical Investigations*. This made him aware of Wittgenstein's *Nachlass* as a literary corpus – a body of manuscripts that were worth preserving and presenting exactly as the author had transmitted them. Like Rhees, von Wright would read Wittgenstein's remarks every day, but unlike Rhees, he no longer wanted to build his *editorial* work on this *philosophical* reading.[230] Von Wright instead began concentrating on the 'externalities', as he put it.[231] He employed two assistants at the Academy of Finland, Heikki Nyman and André Maury, to systematically type out the four then-known pre-versions of the *Philosophical Investigations*. A single page was devoted to each remark, including all of Wittgenstein's variants.[232] The resulting typescript – the so-called Helsinki Edition – was not published but was distributed among interested colleagues.[233] Nyman and Maury then cross-referenced the remarks in the different versions and von Wright synthesized the findings into a second historical study on the composition of the *Philosophical Investigations*.[234]

Von Wright's historical philology not only spurred like-minded young scholars, but also incited criticism of the literary executors' previous volumes. Von Wright was increasingly convinced that 'a thorough revision of the bulk of already published writings' would be called for and he, together with Rhees, revised the *Remarks on the Foundations of Mathematics*.[235] Von Wright also agreed with Kenny's criticism of Rhees's editing and eventually questioned the

---

[227] TLP 1961, cf. Harré, 'Ryle and the Tractatus', 39–53.

[228] See Section 3.4 in the present Element. Other important dimensions of Wittgenstein scholarship originating from Oxford are the very influential commentaries with extensive use of the *Nachlass*. See Hacker and Baker, *Analytical Commentary*.

[229] PT 1971; Wright, *Mitt Liv*, p. 162.   [230] Maury, 'Interview'.

[231] Von Wright, *Wittgenstein*, p. 11.   [232] Ibid, 7–10.

[233] Stern, 'Availability', 464–5; the 'Helsinki Edition' was the basis for PU 2001. See Section 6.4 in the present Element.

[234] Wright, 'Origin and Composition', 111–36; cf. Maury, 'Sources of Zettel', 57–74; and Maury, 'Sources of Philosophical Investigations', 349–78.

[235] RFM 1974 and RFM 1978; Wright, 'Wittgenstein Papers', 60; Wright, 'Correspondence with Rhees', 1971–2.

warranty of Anscombe's and Rhees's decision to include Part II in the *Philosophical Investigations* – although out of respect for Rhees, he did not do so publicly while the latter was still alive.[236]

5.3 Philological Criticism II: Oxford and Tübingen Become Allies

Besides Helsinki and Oxford, the University of Tübingen became a third prominent place for text-critical discussions of the books published from Wittgenstein's *Nachlass*. In Germany in the 1970s, young philologists were inspired by Dietrich Sattler's monumental ambition to critically edit Hölderlin's complete works. They championed principles of historical-critical editing that went against the principles of expert intuition used by an older generation of editors in the scholarly establishment.[237] In Tübingen, this movement joined forces with the university's department for data processing, creating an intellectual atmosphere in which a group of diverse scholars began thinking about producing a computer-based transcription of Wittgenstein's *Nachlass*.[238] This idea first arose in a reading circle established by the Italian theologian Michele Ranchetti, who was then conducting research at Tübingen.

Ranchetti was fascinated by the remarks of Wittgenstein that he discovered in the volumes edited by Rhees. He even translated some of the volumes into Italian and wanted to use the Cornell microfilm to produce new books.[239] However, Ranchetti was an old-fashioned 'analogue' humanist who had no knowledge of technical requirements. He therefore approached Michael Nedo, who was in the reading circle. Nedo organized the research technology at a Max Planck Institute for bio-acoustics.[240] He, Ranchetti and Mario Rosso, one of Ranchetti's doctoral students, began talking about a complete machine-readable transcription and they found the right professor at Tübingen to turn this dream into a research proposal. This was Jürgen Heringer, a linguist who had studied Wittgenstein in Heidelberg and who saw a promising use of Wittgenstein's *Nachlass* for developing algorithms to automatically identify similarities in texts.[241] They approached Rhees about this idea. Rhees was not sure what to make of it and probably felt relieved when the grant proposal eventually failed in late 1975.[242]

Regardless of the fate of the grant proposal, Nedo had devoted himself to the task of editing Wittgenstein's writings. He moved to Cambridge. With a personal fellowship from the German Thyssen Foundation, he aimed to

---

[236] Wright, 'Troubled History', 181–92; Wright, 'Correspondence with Rhees', 15 March 1982.

[237] Hölderlin, *Sämtliche Werke*; cf. Groddeck, Martens, Reuß and Straengle, 'Gespräch', 1–55.

[238] Erbacher, 'Drama', 8–9.

[239] Ibid. 8. For one of Ranchetti's translations, see Ranchetti, *Lezioni*.

[240] Erbacher, 'Drama', 9.   [241] Ibid, 11.   [242] Ibid, 13.

produce a new and uncensored microfilm of Wittgenstein's *Nachlass*.[243] Nedo's work in Cambridge had the blessing of the literary executors and it brought him to the attention of the Oxford Wittgenstein scholars. After some time, the Thyssen Foundation encouraged him to submit a new proposal for a big research project.[244] To prepare that, Nedo invited most of the new Oxford Wittgenstein scholars to a symposium at Tübingen in the spring of 1977.

At the symposium in Tübingen, the challenges of editing Wittgenstein's writings were discussed and a complete edition rendered from a 'computerised database' was envisioned, one that should ensure the exclusion of editors' interpretations.[245] Kenny believed this 'marked the beginning of a new phase in Wittgenstein studies'.[246] Rhees, however, thought that 'most of the self-righteous horror of "*interpretation*" – both in Tübingen and in Oxford – is confused, and often eine Sophisterei [a sophist's trick]'.[247] But von Wright was able to mediate between the conflicting views and convinced Rhees to support the new proposal. This time it was accepted.[248] Shortly afterwards, in the autumn of 1978, the Wittgenstein Archive at the University of Tübingen was inaugurated.[249]

5.4 The Collapse of the Tübingen Archive

The Wittgenstein Archive at the University of Tübingen started with great hopes. It was managed by a group of six men: Nedo and Heringer were the leaders, Ranchetti and McGuinness were expert consultants and Rosso and Schulte were affiliated fellows.[250] In addition, the scientific coordinator Reinhard Nowak supervised a handful of transcribers who had soon made considerable progress.[251] Before long, however, it was evident that the project had too little funding and too little time to fulfil the great task of producing a complete transcription of 20,000 pages.[252] To extend the project, a second Wittgenstein symposium was organized in the summer of 1979.

The second Wittgenstein symposium in Tübingen would be remembered as a high point of the whole project. It gathered the 'who's who' of then-current Wittgenstein scholarship and provided a first-class environment for a week of talks and discussions.[253] In the end, it served its main purpose: the literary executors granted the Tübingen group the exclusive right to create a historical-critical edition of Wittgenstein's writings. It was to be produced under the aegis of the Academy of Sciences in Heidelberg.[254] This great prospect, however, never materialized. For just when it was most needed, the trust between the project group members deteriorated, and they feared they were not working

[243] Ibid, 13–14.   [244] Ibid, 14–15.   [245] Kenny, 'Brief History', 345.   [246] Ibid.
[247] Wright, 'Correspondence with Rhees', 20 April 1977, published in Erbacher, 'Drama', 16.
[248] Ibid, 18–19.   [249] Ibid.   [250] Ibid, 19.   [251] Ibid, 20.   [252] Ibid, 20–1.   [253] Ibid, 24.
[254] Ibid, 25.

towards the same goal. Nedo was mostly in Cambridge. Those who worked in Tübingen felt increasingly uninformed about what he was actually doing; they began to suspect he would pursue his own aims.[255]By the same token, as the plans for a big editorial project within the Academy of Sciences in Heidelberg became more concrete, Nedo saw the project developing in a direction he did not support.[256]

In April 1980, this latent conflict broke out into the open and the Tübingen group wanted Nedo to step down from his position as leader. A letter to this effect was sent to the literary executors.[257] These, in turn, were irritated and feared that the work in Tübingen was out of control. German professors also expressed doubts about the group's competence and von Wright learned that coded remarks had apparently leaked out of the Tübingen Archive and been made public.[258] To find out more, Anscombe and Rhees attended a meeting of the group in Oxford, where plans for an edition with a learned commentary were discussed.[259] Such an edition Anscombe would never allow; she wanted the group to abstain from this aim.[260] Since the group refused, it lost Anscombe's trust. She and Rhees called on the president of Tübingen University to close the archive.[261]

The chancellor and the president of Tübingen University would later travel to Cambridge in an attempt to rescue the project under new management, but to no avail.[262] When the archive was shut down for good, rumours about its dissolution spread in German academia more than did any of the project's scholarly results. This significantly impeded Wittgenstein studies in Germany.

5.5 Cold War in Editing Wittgenstein

The deterioration of trust in the Tübingen Archive did not leave Wittgenstein's literary executors unaffected: von Wright was informed only afterwards about Anscombe's and Rhees's request to shut down the Tübingen Archive and he complained that he would not have agreed to such extreme measures.[263] This was just a slight dissonance between the three at first, but it was amplified when Anscombe vehemently refused to continue working with Blackwell, which had published the Wittgenstein books for more than thirty years.[264] The reason for her refusal was a deterioration of trust after a disagreement over royalties. Von Wright urged both Anscombe and Rhees to bring to completion the set of volumes as edited by the three of them, since only the second volume of *Last Writings on the Philosophy of Psychology* remained to be published.[265] But

---

[255] Ibid, 26–7.   [256] Ibid.   [257] Ibid, 28.   [258] Ibid, 30.   [259] Ibid, 31.   [260] Ibid.
[261] Ibid, 31–2.   [262] Ibid, 33–4.
[263] Wright, 'Correspondence with McGuinness', 6 March 1981; Wright, 'Correspondence with Anscombe', 3 June 1981.
[264] Wright, 'Correspondence with Anscombe', 1982–83.   [265] LW 1992.

even though it was ready for print in 1982, it would take another ten years before Anscombe gave her imprimatur.

Anscombe and Rhees – the latter not comprehending Anscombe's falling out with Blackwell – supported Nedo in his application for funding in order to complete his historical-critical edition of Wittgenstein's writings.[266] This, however, proved to be an endurance test, for the funding was interrupted several times and Nedo's visible progress was excessively slow. He sought perfection in designing a format for Wittgenstein's writings; he experimented with typesetting and even had a special font designed.[267] The first five volumes of the resulting 'Vienna Edition' therefore did not appear before the mid-1990s.[268]

Von Wright experienced these years after the breakdown of the Tübingen Archive as a 'via dolorosa'.[269] He began to feel that the literary executors would betray Wittgenstein's will. Rhees fatalistically added that they would resemble a 'triangle whose interior angles would never sum up to 180°'.[270] Without Anscombe's consent, there was no possibility to publish new editions from Wittgenstein's writings.[271] Hence, von Wright devoted his time to consolidating what had been published thus far and he supported others whose work he regarded as decent.

Von Wright continued to cooperate with McGuinness; in editing parts of Wittgenstein's correspondence, the two also cooperated with Schulte, who was translating many of the posthumous publications of Wittgenstein's letters and lectures into German and compiling a volume of shorter writings.[272] Schulte also revised the collected works series for the German publisher Suhrkamp, and, again in cooperation with McGuinness, eventually published a philologically enhanced edition of the *Tractatus*.[273] These publications, which would not have been possible without Schulte's continuous concentrated and disciplined work, greatly contributed to maintaining and stimulating interest in Wittgenstein's writings in Germany, in spite of the disaster of Tübingen and the moratorium in the literary executors' cooperation.

5.6 The Lives of Wittgenstein

Although there was stagnation in the production of new books from Wittgenstein's *Nachlass* during the 1980s, work on biographical accounts was

---

[266] Wright, 'Correspondence with Anscombe' 1982–8; Wright, 'Correspondence with Rhees', 1982–8.
[267] Nedo, 'Interview'.   [268] Wi1-5.   [269] Wright, *Mitt Liv*, p. 163.
[270] Wright, 'Correspondence with Rhees', 4 December 1982; this seems to be an allusion to Penrose's impossible triangle. See Penrose, 'Impossible Objects', 31–3.
[271] Cf. Wright, 'Correspondence with Anscombe', April–June 1981.
[272] LFM 1976; WWK 1979; CB 1980; AWL 1984; LWL 1984, YB 1979, MDC 1987, PGL 1988.
[273] Werkausgabe 1–8; TLP 1989.

in full bloom. Wittgenstein's secluded and unusual lifestyle had always been an object of rumour at Cambridge and misleading accounts were published or in preparation shortly after his death.[274] Already at that time, the literary executors felt obliged to intervene.[275] This was also the case when, in 1973, William Bartley made allegations about Wittgenstein's homosexual practices.[276] This, of course, aroused much curiosity, but also made it seem as though the literary executors were manipulating the public image of Wittgenstein. The same tune was sung when an unauthorized book entitled *Geheime Tagebücher* [Secret Diaries] was published. This book presented the coded remarks in Wittgenstein's notebooks from World War I, which Anscombe and von Wright had excluded from their publications.[277] Wilhelm Baum had copied them at the Tübingen Archive and made transcripts available without the literary executors being aware of his plan.[278]

But there were also many reliable historical documents, volumes of recollections and letters that had come to light since Wittgenstein's death – Rhees himself had just edited a set of recollections from friends.[279] Hence, the literary executors were not the only ones who would have liked to read a decent biography. Another factor fed this desire as well: people began to see that a substantial connection could be made between Wittgenstein's life and work – not the least through von Wright's publication *Culture and Value,* which includes selected remarks by Wittgenstein on religion, music, architecture and society.[280] Rhees thought that von Wright himself, or Maurice O'Connor Drury, one of Wittgenstein's closest friends, might be able to write a biography, but neither felt suited to the task.[281] But there was one man who had keen insight into the published historical material and who had also discovered and edited some of it: Brian McGuinness.[282] He too was certain that the time was ripe for a biographical account of Wittgenstein and he was willing to undertake the endeavour.[283]

Von Wright supported McGuinness by giving him access to all of his materials and by introducing him to the Wittgenstein family, who gave him a warm welcome as well as frank information.[284] In preparing the biography,

---

[274] Wright, 'Biographical Sketch', 528; cf. Cranston, 'Bildnis', 495–7; Ferrater Mora, 'Destruktion', 489–5; Hayek, 'Biography', 28–82.

[275] Anscombe, 'Letter to the Editor', 97–8; Erbacher, 'First Wittgenstein Biography', 9–26.

[276] Bartley, *Wittgenstein*, pp. 38–40, 47–51; Rhees, 'Wittgenstein', 66–78; Anscombe, 'TLS', X, Monk, *Duty*, pp. 581–6.

[277] See Sections 2.1, 2.5, 4.2, 4.3, 4.5 and 5.4 and A.1 in the present Element.

[278] GT 1985a/b, GT 1991; Baum, *Weltkrieg*, p. 35.   [279] Rhees, *Recollections*.

[280] VB 1977, VB 1980, VB 1994 and VB 1998, See Section 4.3 in the present Element.

[281] Wright, *Wittgenstein*, p. 2; Wright, 'Correspondence with Rhees', 20 February 1967.

[282] For instance: CPE 1967, WLP 1976, WWK 1967, PT 1971.   [283] McGuinness, 'Interview'.

[284] McGuinness, *Young Ludwig*, pp. ix–x; McGuinness, 'Interview'.

McGuinness dedicated so much heart, mind and scholarly scrutiny to it that he took nearly as long to write its first part as 'it took Wittgenstein to live it'.[285] However, shortly after *Young Ludwig* was published in 1988, a second, full biography came out: Ray Monk's vivid *Duty of Genius* was so widely read that McGuinness did not feel it was necessary to complete the second part of his own account of Wittgenstein's life.[286] Despite not publishing a second volume, McGuinness's collection of sources and his studies of episodes in Wittgenstein's life after the *Tractatus* preserve the fascinating multiplicity of his character in a way that one monograph alone could hardly achieve.[287] Just as Wittgenstein's philosophy cannot be paraphrased in a single theory, his life cannot be put into a single biography.

6 Recent Scholarly Editions

6.1 The Norwegian Wittgenstein Project

Unperturbed by what happened in Oxford, Cambridge and Tübingen, another milieu for Wittgenstein scholarship had developed in the north of Europe: in Norway, the country in which Wittgenstein had achieved breakthroughs for both the *Tractatus* (in 1913–14) and the *Philosophical Investigations* (in 1936).[288]

The Norwegian academic interest in Wittgenstein's writings had been largely triggered through the close friendship between von Wright and Knut Erik Tranøy.[289] Tranøy had lived in von Wright's house in Cambridge in the late 1940s and had a career in academic philosophy thereafter. He imported the interest in Wittgenstein to Norway when he became the first philosophy professor at the University of Bergen in 1959.[290] Tranøy's first assistant, Jakob Meløe, became intrigued by the posthumously published writings of Wittgenstein and transmitted his fascination to many students.[291] And there was Viggo Rossvær, who heard about the Cornell microfilm from von Wright.[292] These and other Norwegian scholars joined forces to apply to the Norwegian Research Council for a grant that would enable the four then-existing Norwegian Universities to

---

[285] Hayek, *Draft Biography*, p. 85. McGuinness's Archive has been transferred to the Forschungsinstitut Brenner Archive at the University of Innsbruck.

[286] McGuinness, 'Interview'. Monk's preface suggests that discussions with Rhees were more important for the picture of Wittgenstein drawn in his biography than discussions with von Wright and Anscombe; cf. Monk, *Duty*, p. xii.

[287] For instance: WC 2012; McGuinness, *Approaches*, pp. 3–54 and 177–242. McGuinness, *Schlick*, pp. 41–68.

[288] Cf. Wright, ‚Biographical Sketch', 531, 540; Monk, *Duty*, pp. 91–105.

[289] Wright, *Mitt Liv*, pp. 139–40.   [290] Erbacher, 'Brief', 580–1.

[291] Johannessen, 'Interview'; Nordenstam, 'Interview'.   [292] Rossvær, 'Interview'.

buy and study a copy of the Cornell microfilm.[293] This formed the foundation for the 'Norwegian Wittgenstein Project'.

In the Norwegian Wittgenstein Project, there was also transcription work going on, but the aim of it was merely to gain a readable source, not to publish anything.[294] In 1981, however, Rossvær became acquainted with Nowak, the scientific coordinator of the Tübingen Archive. Rossvær learned about the Tübingen Archive's deterioration when the two men met again in Dubrovnik in 1982.[295] They toyed with the idea of the Norwegians continuing the work that had started in Tübingen. In 1984, Heringer sent an assistant to Norway to hand over magnetic tapes that contained the transcriptions that had already been made at the Wittgenstein Archive in Tübingen.[296] Von Wright supported this development, considering it a great opportunity to complete the transcription of the *Nachlass*.[297] However, since Anscombe supported Nedo's editorial ambition, she would not consent to any transcription being done in Norway unless the tapes from Tübingen were handed over to Nedo. This the Norwegians had promised *not* to do.[298] There was thus an impasse; the work of transcribing Wittgenstein's writings in Norway effectively came to an halt.

In 1985, a new leader of the Norwegian Wittgenstein Project, Claus Huitfeldt, tried to solve the problem in order to continue transcribing Wittgenstein's writings in Norway. Leading international scholars supported this initiative with a conference in Skibotn, Norway, in 1986, and with a formal petition in 1987.[299] The Norwegians repeatedly invited Anscombe to Norway with the aim of winning her consent.[300] But all efforts were in vain; she would not agree to anything unless the magnetic tapes containing the transcriptions made at Tübingen were handed over to Nedo. Huitfeldt undertook a last diplomatic journey to the UK in early 1988, meeting with Rhees, Nedo and Anscombe.[301] This wholehearted attempt also failed to change Anscombe's mind and the Norwegian Wittgenstein Project had to be 'frozen down'.[302]

6.2 A Solomonic Decision

In 1989, the first of Wittgenstein's literary executors died. Rhees was concerned with Wittgenstein's papers until the very last moments of his conscious life and gave his wife orders that von Wright ought to take his (Rhees's) Wittgenstein

---

[293] Huitfeldt and Rossvær, *Norwegian Wittgenstein Project*, pp. 6–16.   [294] Ibid, pp. 6–9.

[295] Nowak, 'Wittgenstein Archive', 28 April 1982; Rossvær, 'Interview'.

[296] Huitfeldt and Rossvær, *Norwegian Wittgenstein Project*, p. 10.

[297] Wright, 'Correspondence with Rhees', 1984–6; Wright, 'Correspondence with Anscombe', 1984–6.

[298] Huitfeldt and Rossvær, *Norwegian Wittgenstein Project*, p. 10.   [299] Ibid, pp. 13, 240.

[300] Nordenstam, 'Interview'.

[301] Huitfeldt and Rossvær, *Norwegian Wittgenstein Project*, pp. 14, 257–73.   [302] Ibid, p. 15.

material to the Wren Library at Trinity College Cambridge.[303] When
Wittgenstein's papers had been deposited there in 1969, it had been agreed
that the literary executors would appoint successors who would consult the
Wren in questions of publishing.[304] Peter Winch thus succeeded Rhees and
became secretary to the trustees.[305]

In Winch's correspondence and in the minutes that he kept of the trustees'
meetings, there is documentation of the negotiations that eventually led to
a resolution of the deadlock between Cambridge and Norway.[306] The problem's
resolution was prepared through von Wright's decision to appoint his own
successor; he chose Kenny, who not only shared von Wright's view on how to
edit Wittgenstein's papers, but who was also Anscombe's respected friend and
discussion partner since the time he had worked on his DPhil thesis.[307] Being
a suitable mediator, Kenny was sent to inspect Nedo's work. He proposed
a Solomonic decision: he approved of the high quality of the editorial work
that Nedo had carried out during the past decade and believed that this work
ought to be made available; at the same time, however, he suggested that the
scope of Nedo's work should be limited to the writings of Wittgenstein's middle
period and that the people in Norway should be allowed to produce an electronic
transcription of all of Wittgenstein's writings.[308] This was a resolution everyone
agreed to. Consequently, Nedo could publish a critical edition of writings from
the first half of the 1930s and the Norwegians could create an electronic
transcription of the entire *Nachlass*.

One might assume that the compromise reached between the trustees
would solve the problems for Nedo's Vienna Edition, but alas, it was not
to be. Partly because there had been much trouble with funding and finding
a suitable publisher, the first volumes of the Vienna Edition did not appear
until 1994.[309] Nedo's critics and also von Wright could then be convinced
that Nedo had produced faithful transcriptions and that he had invented
a complex editorial apparatus for variants, corrections and connections to
other items in Wittgenstein's *Nachlass*.[310] But in spite of Nedo's workman-
ship, the Vienna Edition has not become a standard reference in
Wittgenstein scholarship. This may not solely be due to the unwieldiness
of the beautiful and well-crafted volumes, but mainly due to the conflicts

---

[303] Wright, 'Correspondence with Rhees', 5 July 1989; cf. 'Rhees Papers' at the Wren Library.

[304] Wright, 'Wittgenstein Papers', 39. See Section 4.5 in the present Element.

[305] Wright, 'Correspondence with Anscombe', 9 July 1989; Wright, *Mitt Liv*, p. 166.

[306] A box with documents archived by Winch and succeeding secretaries to the board of trustees is
kept at the Wren Library.

[307] Kenny, 'Brief History', 347–8; Kenny, *A Life*, p. 15; cf. Wright, 'Correspondence with Kenny',
1974–2002.

[308] Kenny, 'Interview'.   [309] Wi1-5.   [310] Wright, *Mitt Liv*, p. 166; Paul, *Progress*, p. 8.

from which they originated.[311] This reveals a major difference between Nedo's project and the Norwegian project, which was now – with broad support from the community of Wittgenstein scholars – ready to start anew on creating an electronic transcription.

6.3 The Wittgenstein Archives at the University of Bergen

With the founding of the Wittgenstein Archives at the University of Bergen (WAB) in 1990, Claus Huitfeldt revived the Norwegian Wittgenstein Project and gave it a clear objective: to create a complete machine-readable transcription of Wittgenstein's *Nachlass*.[312] Both Anscombe and von Wright now supported this endeavour, even though they had no knowledge of the technological requirements involved.[313] Huitfeldt, by contrast, did have a clue.

Huitfeldt had experimented with electronic transcriptions of Wittgenstein's writings ever since he had first been employed for that purpose when doing his national service (in lieu of military service). He was also in contact with the Text Encoding Initiative (the TEI Consortium) that was in the process of establishing the future Extensible Markup Language (XML) standards for encoding documents in a format readable by people as well as machines.[314] Having started at the bottom and being in touch with the frontiers of text encoding, Huitfeldt created a markup language especially for Wittgenstein's writings and, for that matter, for any similarly complex documents.[315] To implement and elaborate on the code, Alois Pichler was hired in the early 1990s. Pichler, a young philosopher and philologist from the University of Innsbruck, was well-suited and prepared for the task, as he had studied under Allan Janik, who, in turn, was in close contact with the professors at the University of Bergen who stood behind the Wittgenstein Archives. Pichler therefore became the WAB's first paid employee. The WAB soon attracted researchers from abroad, who came to study the *Nachlass* and to discuss its digital transcription.[316] These two features – the developing of digital tools for editing Wittgenstein and being

---

[311] Kenny, 'Brief History', 353–4; Hintikka, 'Impatient Man'. See Sections 5.4 and 5.5 in the present Element.

[312] Wittgenstein Archives, 'Report 1990', 29.

[313] Huitfeldt, 'Interview'. The solution to the impasse, due to the magnetic tapes from Tübingen, was reached thus: Huitfeldt donated the tapes to the University Library of Bergen with the stipulation that they were not to be shown to anyone. Since then, the tapes have not been looked at.

[314] Pichler and Krüger, 'Interview'. An archive with an extensive collection of documents from the WAB's history, including its predecessor the 'Norwegian Wittgenstein Project', has been established at the University of Bergen.

[315] Wittgenstein Archives, 'Report 1990–1993', 24–8; Huitfeldt, 'Machine-Readable Version'; Huitfeldt, 'Multi-Dimensional Texts'.

[316] Wittgenstein Archives, 'Report 1990–1993', 36, 60–3; Pichler and Krüger, 'Interview'.

a hospitable place for lively research and discussion – have characterized the WAB ever since.[317]

After four years, WAB's coding and transcription work was evaluated, with the result that its funding was extended.[318] It was now possible to form a larger team consisting of scholars who were not only familiar with Wittgenstein's writings but also with editing philosophical texts and text linguistics, in order to pursue a more ambitious goal: the publication of a complete electronic edition.[319] Kenny, who was Pro-Vice-Chancellor of the University of Oxford at that time, helped organize an arrangement with Oxford University Press, which agreed to work with the WAB in exploring this new digital form of publishing. It required intense effort from everyone involved, but eventually six CD-ROMs were launched in 2000, providing a complete transcription of *Wittgenstein's Nachlass* in normalized and diplomatic form as well as a full set of digitized facsimiles.[320] What is more, being equipped with multiple and detailed search functions, this *Bergen Electronic Edition* (BEE) allows for tracing variants of remarks in Wittgenstein's oeuvre.

The BEE, in its completeness and simplicity, represents a milestone in editing Wittgenstein. It is a success story in early digital humanities. However, the rapid changes in software and operating systems have required a constant elaboration of the edition and an eventual shift to a flexible web-based version.[321] Much progress on this has already been made, through Pichler's ongoing effort to create synergies between editing Wittgenstein and digitizing philosophy.[322]

6.4 Half a Century after Wittgenstein's Death

The computerization of Wittgenstein's texts at the Wittgenstein Archives in Bergen was the last milestone Anscombe experienced in the history of editing her teacher's writings. She suffered a car crash, struggled with injuries for some time and died in 2001.[323] Von Wright, now well over eighty years old, would live to see yet another editorial milestone: the *Critical-Genetic Edition* of the *Philosophical Investigations*.[324]

---

[317] See the WAB's website for a history of guest researchers. The current director Alois Pichler tends to say that the WAB owns no originals except its guestbook.

[318] Wittgenstein Archives, 'Report 1990–1993', 67–107.

[319] Wittgenstein Archives, 'Report 1995', 17–19.

[320] BEE; the 'normalized' transcription offers a clean reading version of the text, while the 'diplomatic' version aims to preserve all text phenomena such as Wittgenstein's deletions, underlinings or use of code.

[321] www.wittgensteinsource.org.

[322] Pichler, 'New Bergen Electronic Edition', 57–172; Pichler and Bruvik, 'Digital Critical Editing', 179–99.

[323] Geach, 'Letter to von Wright', 28 February 2001.

[324] PU 2001. See Section 5.2 in the present Element. The publication of Will in 2000 was also of great importance to von Wright.

Following in the steps of von Wright's historical research on the *Nachlass*, Schulte had elaborated the so-called *Helsinki-Edition* in order to prepare a text-critical edition of the *Philosophical Investigations*.[325] The resulting *Critical-Genetic Edition* provides, in historical sequence, five versions of the *Philosophical Investigations*, namely the *Ur-Version* from 1936, the *Early Version* from 1937–8, the *Revised Early Version* from 1939–44, the *Intermediate Version* from 1944–5 and the *Late Version* from 1945–6.[326] In each of these versions, Wittgenstein's revisions and variants are notated, so that the genesis of the work can be studied both within and in between the versions.

In many respects, the *Critical-Genetic Edition* combines the three editorial approaches Wittgenstein's literary executors developed: Anscombe's conviction that it was important to focus on Wittgenstein's main works (i.e. the *Tractatus* and *Philosophical Investigations*), Rhees's insight that it was essential to follow the internal development of that work within the *Nachlass*, and von Wright's example of historically reconstructing the work process and how it materialized in the written documents. The *Critical-Genetic Edition* also reveals clashes between these three approaches: Anscombe's and Rhees's decision regarding the typescript that they had included as Part II in their edition of *Philosophical Investigations* had already been questioned by von Wright, for he had not found written justification for its inclusion.[327] Schulte dealt with this by writing 'Part II' in inverted commas and by publishing a manuscript that is considered to be the last existing pre-version of the typescript that Anscombe and Rhees used for printing Part II – the typescript itself was lost after the printing in 1953.[328] Prefacing Schulte's edition, von Wright addressed the issue for the last time.[329]

The *Critical-Genetic Edition* thus marks approximately fifty years of editing Wittgenstein's writings. The endeavour began with Anscombe's and Rhees's canonical translation and publication of the *Philosophical Investigation* in 1953 and Schulte, in 2001, completed the text-critical and historical work that von Wright had begun, namely, to reconstruct the origin and composition of the book. This in turn was the basis for Schulte's and Peter Hacker's revised translation.[330] For both the *Critical-Genetic Edition* and the new translation of the *Philosophical Investigations,* the editors achieved their goal by standing on the shoulders, as it were, of all the previous editors of Wittgenstein's papers – editors who strove to make Wittgenstein's writings available in a faithful and

---

[325] PU 2001, 44–7. See Section 5.2 in the present Element.

[326] See Sections 1.2, 1.3, 1.4, 2.1, 3.2 and 5.2 and A.5, A.6 and A.8 in the present Element.

[327] Wright, 'Troubled History'. See Sections 1.3, 1.4 and 5.2 in the present Element.

[328] See Sections 1.3 and A.9 in the present Element.   [329] PU 2001, 7–11.

[330] PI 2009; Schulte, 'Die Revision', 173–94.

surveyable form. This striving constitutes a common tradition, in spite of the disagreements, challenges and even at times despair that accompanied it.[331] And the tradition became a legacy when von Wright, the last remaining literary heir, died in 2003.[332]

6.5 Editions as Readings

The story of Wittgenstein's *Nachlass* is a happy one. In trying to fulfil the task set in Wittgenstein's will, Rhees, Anscombe and von Wright created books that have entered the philosophical canon as Wittgenstein's works. The tradition they started – of making Wittgenstein's thinking available to the public – has been going on now for more than sixty years. One of the most recent steps in this living tradition is that Wittgenstein's *Nachlass* has been included in UNESCO's Memory of the World Register.[333]

In this book, I have discussed the first six decades in the history of editing Wittgenstein – from Wittgenstein's death in 1951 to the death of the last original literary heir in 2003. Looking back over this account, it is possible to identify three paradigmatic phases: a philosophical phase, a critical phase and a post-critical phase.

First, when preparing their books, Rhees, Anscombe and von Wright followed Wittgenstein's wish by following their own judgement. They were well-trained by their teacher, as readers of his writings and as philosophers in their own right. Thus, they let their philosophical understanding of Wittgenstein's writings govern their editing, with the aim of making available, in the most accessible way, what they thought Wittgenstein's philosophy was. Their editorial work can thus be called the 'philosophical phase' in the history of editing Wittgenstein's writings.

Second, having access to the Cornell microfilm, scholars found that Rhees, Anscombe and von Wright had intervened more strongly in the selection and composition of the books than their austere prefaces and epilogues indicated. This led to a second, 'critical' phase characterized by editors who did not know Wittgenstein personally and who wanted to produce publications from the *Nachlass* strictly according to philological principles. This text-critical examination led to three editorial branches that are still flourishing: first, printed critical editions, such as the *Critical-Genetic Edition* of the *Philosophical Investigations*, second, the *Vienna Edition*, which is a critical edition of Wittgenstein's writings up to the mid-1930s and, third, the *Bergen Electronic Edition*, which provides the complete writings of Wittgenstein in diplomatic

---

[331] Erbacher, 'Philosophical Reasons', 140–1.
[332] Wallgren and Österman, 'Archives', 273–82.   [333] See www.unesco.org.

and normalized transcriptions as well as in facsimile. The BEE is on the way to becoming freely available online.[334] All surviving writings by Wittgenstein will therefore, in principle, be accessible to interested readers.

Third, the new availabilities resulting from the critical phase require that readers develop heightened interpretative capacities. As a consequence of the increasing (digital) availability of Wittgenstein's papers, readers are empowered to explore, restructure and display Wittgenstein's writings according to their own individual needs. With this empowerment, however, readers are confronted with questions of composition and internal relations. Before digitization, such questions had been dealt with only by selected and trained editors, but when new readers are confronted with the same questions, they can gain help and an orientation in Wittgenstein's writings through insights into the reasons and motives for the different modes of previous editing. In this way, the various editions no longer need to be judged merely as candidates for canonization, but can be appreciated as achievements by outstanding readers of the source material. This new perspective in studying editorial work on Wittgenstein's *Nachlass* is characteristic for the third phase in the history of editing Wittgenstein's writings; it is a 'post-critical' phase that supplies the critical editorial philology with an additional hermeneutical adventure, thus enabling today's readers to understand Wittgenstein's writings under the conditions of the first editors' understanding and thereby understand the meaning of editing in the context of philosophical inheritance. The present book has been an attempt to stimulate future adventures of this kind.

---

[334] www.wittgensteinsource.org.

Appendix
Looking into Wittgenstein's Nachlass

This book tells the story of the posthumous editing of Wittgenstein's writings, yet without delving into philological technicalities. Anyone who wants to look at the actual manuscripts and typescripts that Wittgenstein left to posterity – to become fascinated by tracing the ways in which they came into being and to investigate in greater detail how they relate to the published volumes that Wittgenstein's heirs and editors created – may consult the documents digitally. They are fully available in electronic form through the *Bergen Electronic Edition*[1] and, to a great extent, online at www.wittgensteinsource.org. A few prominent manuscripts and typescripts will be briefly introduced in the following paragraphs in order to illustrate the questions that Wittgenstein's heirs and editors have had to deal with. The brief discussions may also be of benefit to first-time users of the available electronic resources and to those who are interested in carrying out further philosophical-philological studies. The documents are referred to by the number they have been assigned in von Wright's catalogue[2] and through the permanent web address at www .wittgensteinsource.org. They are discussed here in the chronological order of their creation.

A.1 Ms 101, www.wittgensteinsource.org/BFE/Ms-101_f[3]

Ms 101 is one of the notebooks that Wittgenstein wrote during World War I. He was twenty-five years of age when the war broke out in 1914 and he volunteered for the Austrian Army. During his service he kept working on what would become the *Tractatus*. Three of his notebooks from this period have survived: Ms 101, Ms 102 and Ms 103. In writing them, Wittgenstein did his philosophical work on the right-hand side of each page and used the left-hand sides for diary-like entries, writing them in a special code that was an inversion of the alphabet. When Anscombe and von Wright edited the war notebooks, publishing them as *Notebooks 1914–1916*,[4] they only printed the right-hand sides. This was because they thought the coded entries were irrelevant for understanding Wittgenstein's philosophy. By contrast, many of today's scholars regard the

---

[1] BEE 2000.

[2] Wright, 'Wittgenstein Papers'; updates of the catalogue have been published in Wright, *Wittgenstein*; PO 1993; BEE; PPO 2003 and on www.wittgensteinonline.no

[3] See Sections 2.1, 2.5, 4.2, 4.3, 4.5, 5.4 and 5.6 in the present Element.   [4] TB 1961.

coded remarks not only as interesting contextual information on the conditions under which parts of the *Tractatus* were written, but also as belonging to Wittgenstein's philosophical oeuvre.[5] In 1991, Wilhelm Baum, without the literary executors' permission, published the left-hand sides of all three war notebooks, calling them Wittgenstein's 'secret diaries'.[6] In this publication, the coded entries were removed from their philosophical context just as the uncoded ones were removed from their life-world context in Anscombe and von Wright's edition. A new edition that presents both sides of the war notebooks in juxtaposition will be available shortly.

A.2 Ts 209, www.wittgensteinsource.org/BFE/Ts-209_f[7]

Ts 209 is the first large collection of remarks Wittgenstein composed after he resumed philosophical writing in 1929. To create it, Wittgenstein first typed selections of remarks from his notebooks and then cut out single passages from the resulting typescript. After this he arranged them anew by gluing them into a ledger. Rhees believed that Wittgenstein gave this ledger to Bertrand Russell in connection with an application to renew his fellowship at Cambridge University.[8] More recent investigations have argued that Wittgenstein did not give this collection to Russell but its source, namely, the typescript Ts 208.[9] In any case, G. E. Moore had the ledger (Ts 209) in his possession at the time of Wittgenstein's death and, in accordance with Wittgenstein's wish, turned it over to the literary executors. Henceforth, this collection was called the 'Moore volume'. Today, only a photocopy of the original Moore volume exists because Rhees accidentally left the original in a telephone booth at Paddington Station in 1962.[10] Luckily, he had already produced a microfilm copy from which he subsequently edited *Philosophical Remarks*.[11] This publication contains the edited text of Ts 209, but also a preface from 1930 as well as material by Wittgenstein that was found among the papers in Friedrich Waismann's estate. Rhees also divided the text into chapters and sections and added an analytical index. This long-winding path – leading from Wittgenstein's creation and through the subsequent editorial history – makes Ts 209 an example of how Wittgenstein worked and how his literary executors handled their inheritance.

[5] Somavilla, 'Coded Remarks', 30–50.   [6] GT 1991.
[7] See Sections 2.1, 2.3, 3.3, 3.4, 3.5, 4.2 and 4.5 in the present Element.
[8] PB 1964; PB 1975.   [9] Pichler, *Untersuchungen*, pp. 53–9; MWL 2016, xxxi–xxxv.
[10] Rhees, 'Letter to von Wright', 26 July 1962, published in Erbacher, Jung and Seibel, 'Logbook', 111–13.
[11] PB 1964, first English edition: PB 1975.

A.3

Ts 213, www.wittgensteinsource.org/BFE/Ts-213_f;

Ms 114, www.wittgensteinsource.org/BFE/Ms-114_f;

Ms 115, www.wittgensteinsource.org/BFE/Ms-115_f;

Ms 140, www.wittgensteinsource.org/BFE/Ms-114_f[12]

This is a set of items stemming from 1933–4 that Rhees edited while producing *Philosophical Grammar*.[13] Rhees's initial idea was to edit the so-called Big Typescript (Ts 213). While working on this, he found two manuscripts (Ms 114 second part and Ms 115 first part) that contained the very same text he himself had already obtained by carrying out Wittgenstein's handwritten corrections in the Big Typescript. However, while editing the newly discovered 'Revision' of the Big Typescript, he found a 'Second Revision' (Ms 140), which he then took into account as well. The result is that there is no single item in Wittgenstein's *Nachlass* that would equal the text of *Philosophical Grammar*. Anthony Kenny's account of the differences between this volume and the Big Typescript heightened scholars' awareness of possible discrepancies between Wittgenstein's papers and the volumes edited from them.[14] At the same time, the controversy shows how difficult it is to decide what can justifiably be called a work by Wittgenstein.[15]

A.4 Ms 115, www.wittgensteinsource.org/BFE/Ms-115_f[16]

The second part of Ms 115, which begins on page 118 of the manuscript, contains Wittgenstein's translation of the so-called *Brown Book*. This was a candidate for a book conception that Wittgenstein dictated to two students and friends in 1934–5. At the end of the following year, he secluded himself in his cabin in Norway and began translating the text into German. He ploughed through a great number of pages, but when he got to page 292 he stopped, saying the whole attempt would be worthless. This resulted in a peculiar situation: the published English version of the *Brown Book* is by Wittgenstein, and the German version is partly translated by a scholar.[17] The same holds true for the other dictation that Rhees published together with the *Brown Book*: the *Blue Book* was dictated to students to supplement Wittgenstein's classes in 1933–4.

---

[12] See Sections 2.4 and 5.1 in the present Element.   [13] PG 1969, cf. Wi11, iix.

[14] Kenny, 'To the *Philosophical Grammar*'.   [15] Schulte, 'Work?', 397–404.

[16] See Sections 3.2 and 3.5 in the present Element.

[17] BBB 1958. No English translation of the *revised* German edition of the *Brown Book* has as yet been published.

Soon an underground trade in copies of the *Blue Book* developed, which Rhees wanted to bring to a halt. He therefore edited and published an authorized version that was also meant to make clear that both dictations were no more than *Preliminary Studies for the Philosophical Investigations*, which is Rhees's subtitle for the publication.

A.5 Ms 142, www.wittgensteinsource.org/BFE/Ms-142_f[18]

After abandoning the translation of the *Brown Book* in the winter of 1936, Wittgenstein drafted the manuscript Ms 142, which is now known as the very first version of the *Philosophical Investigations*. Wittgenstein dedicated it to his sister, Margarete Stonborough, calling it 'a poor Christmas present'. The text of this beautifully handwritten fair copy contains the first 188 remarks of the published *Philosophical Investigations*.[19] This is the reason why the *Critical-Genetic Edition* regards Ms 142 as the *Ur-Version* of the *Philosophical Investigations* and provides a full transcript of it.[20] The actual manuscript was kept by Wittgenstein's sister, who showed it to von Wright in the summer of 1952.[21] It then went missing for many years, as Wittgenstein's sister had given it as a souvenir to Wittgenstein's friend, Rudolf Koder. In 1992, it was rediscovered among the papers in Koder's estate.[22]

A.6 Ts 226, www.wittgensteinsource.org/BFE/Ts-226_f[23]

Ts 226 51 is Rhees's translation of the *Early Version* of the *Philosophical Investigations* from 1937–8. The great influence which Wittgenstein's philosophy has had in English-speaking academia is surely due to his having been a teacher at Cambridge, but also due to Anscombe's congenial translation of the *Philosophical Investigations*. Wittgenstein cared a lot about the translation of his work and he had been looking for a translator for quite some time before Anscombe became involved. In 1938 he wanted to publish a bilingual book with the title *Philosophische Bemerkungen – Philosophical Remarks*. For this purpose, he tried several candidate translators,[24] from which selection, Rhees was eventually chosen. His translation, however, did not satisfy Wittgenstein and the latter found it necessary to make many corrections and revisions in Rhees's typescript. These corrections are still preserved in Ts 226, which makes the document a valuable aid not only when thinking about possible renderings of Wittgenstein's remarks into English, but also when considering details of

[18] See Sections 1.2, 1.3, 1.4, 2.1, 3.2, 5.2 and 6.4 in the present Element. [19] PI 1953.
[20] PU 2003. [21] Wright, *Mitt Liv*, p. 177. [22] PU 2003, 31.
[23] See Sections 1.4 and 3.1 in the present Element. [24] Redpath, *Memoir*, p. 73.

Anscombe's most influential translation from 1951.[25] Today, there is a revised translation of the *Philosophical Investigations* that is based on the *Critical-Genetic Edition*.[26]

A.7 Ms 125, www.wittgensteinsource.org/BFE/Ms-125_f[27]

Ms 125 was created in 1941–2. This is one of the manuscripts from which Rhees, Anscombe and von Wright selected remarks for their second publication: *Remarks on the Foundations of Mathematics*.[28] This volume contains selections from no fewer than eleven items in Wittgenstein's *Nachlass*, covering the period 1937–44. The editors knew that Wittgenstein's work on the foundations of mathematics had for a long time had a central position in his philosophical thinking, so they chose it to be their next edition following the *Philosophical Investigations*. However, although the literary executors repeatedly decided to select passages from various manuscripts, this editorial approach turned out to be problematic and the printing of Wittgenstein's mathematical symbols and drawings posed practical difficulties as well. *Remarks on the Foundations of Mathematics* is therefore probably the most troublesome of Rhees, Anscombe and von Wright's editing. It is the only book officially co-edited by all three literary executors, and it was significantly revised in 1974, after they had gained a better overview of Wittgenstein's writings.

A.8 Ts 227a, www.wittgensteinsource.org/BFE/Ts-227a_f[29]

Ts 227a is a typescript, composed by Wittgenstein, of the last version of what would be printed as the *Philosophical Investigations*. The typescript stems from the end of 1945 and beginning of 1946. Shortly after Wittgenstein's death in 1951, Anscombe and Rhees prepared another copy of this typescript, as part of the process that led to the publication of the *Philosophical Investigations* in 1953. But since this copy was lost after typesetting, there is no single item in Wittgenstein's *Nachlass* that equals the text of Anscombe and Rhees's publication. The two still-extant copies of the typescript contain partly differing corrections in Wittgenstein's hand (and partly in other hands). This shows that Wittgenstein revised his remarks even in the last existing version. When Anscombe asked Wittgenstein, in 1951, how she ought to choose between the variants, Wittgenstein is said to have replied that she could toss a coin.[30] Even

[25] Schulte, 'Die Revision', 173–94.   [26] PI 2009.
[27] See Sections 2.1, 2.3 and 2.4 in the present Element.   [28] RFM 1956.
[29] See Sections 1.2, 1.3, 1.4, 2.1, 3.2, 5.2 and 6.4 in the present Element.
[30] Nedo, *Einführung*, p. 75.

so, he was eager to tell Rhees, ten days before his death, that 'care should be taken in what was published and how it was presented'.[31] Wittgenstein's revisions in the two still-existing copies of Ts 227 are edited in the *Critical-Genetic Edition* that also presents earlier versions in full text, that is, the *Ur-Fassung* from 1936 (Ms 142), the *Early Version* from 1937–8 (Tss 225, 220, 221), the *Revised Early Version* from 1939–44 (Ts 239), and the *Intermediate Version* from 1944–5 (Ts 242).[32]

A.9 Ms 144, www.wittgensteinsource.org/BFE/Ms-144_f[33]

This manuscript is the last-existing pre-version of the typescript from which Part II of Anscombe and Rhees's publication of the *Philosophical Investigations* (1953) was printed.[34] Just like the typescript for Part I, the typescript for Part II was lost after typesetting. The same is true for a second copy of the typescript.[35] Hence, there is no text in Wittgenstein's *Nachlass* that equals Part II of Anscombe and Rhees's edition of the *Philosophical Investigations*. Ms 144 differs in the sequence of the remarks that – in contrast to the published Part II – are not numbered. But the greatest editorial issue with Part II of the *Philosophical Investigations* from 1953 is not how it was edited, but whether it really belongs there. Anscombe and Rhees included it because of their memories of what Wittgenstein told them in December 1947 about his plans for the book.[36] The typescript they used for Part II, created in 1949, seemed to them to be the most well worked-out form of what they thought Wittgenstein would have wanted to include. But their decision to include this Part II was criticized by von Wright and others.[37]

A.10 Ms 177, www.wittgensteinsource.org/BFE/Ms-177_f[38]

Ms 177 contains the very last remarks that Wittgenstein ever wrote. Until two days before his death, Wittgenstein wrote philosophical remarks into this small notebook. Anscombe and von Wright edited it together with remarks from further manuscripts in a volume that they entitled *On Certainty*.[39] Just as with two other volumes presenting writings from the last months of Wittgenstein's life – *Remarks on Colour*[40] and *Last Writings on the Philosophy of Psychology*[41] – the title is not Wittgenstein's own choice. The editors chose titles they thought would cover the overall theme of the remarks in the edited

---

[31] Erbacher, 'Literary Executors', 30.   [32] PU 2003.
[33] See Sections 1.3, 3.1, 4.1, 5.2, 6.4 in the present Element.   [34] PI 1953; cf. PU 2003, 27–30.
[35] PU 2003, 29.   [36] Erbacher, 'Approaches', 171.
[37] E.g. Wright, 'Troubled History'; Stern, 'Availability'.
[38] See Sections 4.1 and 5.5 in the present Element.   [39] OC 1969.   [40] ROC 1977.
[41] LW 1992.

volumes. This editorial intervention became increasingly questionable the more it became clear that Anscombe and von Wright not only created the titles for the publications, but actually selected the remarks for these volumes from the same set of manuscripts and grouped them in accordance with the titles they themselves had chosen. Although this categorization of the remarks according to topic was partly indicated by Wittgenstein's own marks in the manuscript, Anscombe's and von Wright's editing practice is also very similar to Rhees's in one respect: they intervened heavily in the texts in Wittgenstein's *Nachlass* when editing them and they based their editorial interventions on their own philosophical understanding of the writings they edited. Their work, however, also laid the foundations for creating the textual resources to critically review their achievements.

Bibliography

Publications from Wittgenstein's *Nachlass*, Correspondence and Notes Made in His Lectures

The abbreviations used in this book were introduced in Pichler, Biggs and Szeltner, *Bibliographie*.

AM 1961	'Notes dictated to G. E. Moore in Norway' in G. H. von Wright and G. E. M. Anscombe (eds.), translated by G. E. M. Anscombe, *Notebooks 1914–1916* (Oxford: Basil Blackwell, 1961), pp. 107–18.
AWL 1979	*Wittgenstein's Lectures: Cambridge*, 1932–1935, edited by A. Ambrose (Oxford: Basil Blackwell, 1979).
AWL 1984	'Cambridge 1932–1935', A. Ambrose (ed.), translated by J. Schulte, *Ludwig Wittgenstein. Vorlesungen 1930–1935* (Frankfurt am Main: Suhrkamp, 1984), pp. 141–442.
BBB 1958	*Preliminary Studies for the 'Philosophical Investigations'*, generally known as The Blue and Brown Books (Oxford: Basil Blackwell, 1958).
BEE	*Wittgenstein's Nachlass. The Bergen Electronic Edition*, The Wittgenstein Archives at the University of Bergen (ed.) (Oxford: Oxford University Press, 2000).
BT 2005	*The Big Typescript: TS 213*, edited and translated by C. Grant Luckhardt and M. A. E. Aue (Oxford: Blackwell, 2005).
BTE	Wittgenstein Source Bergen Text Edition (www.wittgensteinsource.org/).
CB 1980	*Briefe*, edited by B. F. McGuinness and G. H. von Wright, translated by J. Schulte (Frankfurt am Main: Suhrkamp, 1980).
CCO 1973	*Letters to C. K. Ogden*, edited and with an introduction by G. H. von Wright and an appendix of letters by F. P. Ramsey (Oxford: Basil Blackwell and London: Routledge & Kegan Paul, 1973).
CEM 1933	'Letter to the Editor', *Mind*, 42 (1933), 415–6; edited in PO 1993, 156–8.

(cont.)

CPE 1967	Engelmann, P., 'Briefe von Wittgenstein/Letters from Wittgenstein' in B. F. McGuinness (ed.), translated by L. Furtmüller, *Letters from Ludwig Wittgenstein. With a Memoir* (Oxford: Basil Blackwell, 1967), pp. 2–59.
CRK 1974	*Letters to Russell, Keynes and Moore*, edited and with an Introduction by G. H. von Wright, assisted by B. F. McGuinness (Oxford: Basil Blackwell, 1974).
DB 1997a	*Denkbewegungen. Tagebücher 1930–1932, 1936–1937,* edited by I. Somavilla, Teil 1: Normalisierte Fassung (Innsbruck: Haymon, 1997).
DB 1997b	*Denkbewegungen. Tagebücher 1930–1932, 1936–1937,* edited by I. Somavilla, Teil 2: Diplomatische Fassung (Innsbruck: Haymon, 1997).
DB 2003	'Movements of Thought: Diaries, 1930–1932, 1936–1937', in J. C. Klagge and A. Nordmann (eds.), *Ludwig Wittgenstein. Public and Private Occasions* (Lanham, Boulder, New York, Oxford: Rowman & Littlefield, 2003), pp. 3–255.
GB 1971	'Remarks on Frazer's Golden Bough', *The Human World,* 3 (1971), pp. 18–41; edited in PO 1993, 115–55.
GESAMTBRIEF-WECHSEL 2011	*Gesamtbriefwechsel – Innsbrucker elektronische Ausgabe, 2nd edition,* edited by A. Coda, G. Citron, B. Halder, A. Janik, U. Lobis, K. Mayr, B. F. McGuinness, M. Schorner, M. Seekircher and J. Wang for the Forschungsinstitut Brenner-Archiv (Charlottesville, VA: InteLex, 2011).
GT 1985a	'Diarios Secretos/Geheime Tagebücher', *Saber,* 5 (1985), 24–49.
GT 1985b	'Diarios Secretos (y II)/Geheime Tagebücher', *Saber,* 6 (1985), 30–59.
GT 1991	*Geheime Tagebücher,* edited by W. Baum (Vienna: Turia und Kant, 1991).
LA 1966	*Lectures and Conversations,* edited by C. Barrett (Oxford: Basil Blackwell, 1966).
LE 1965	'A Lecture on Ethics', in 'Wittgenstein's Lecture on Ethics', *The Philosophical Review,* 74 (1965), 3–12; edited in PO 1993, 36–44.

(cont.)

LFM 1976	*Wittgenstein's Lectures on the Foundations of Mathematics: Cambridge, 1939,* edited by C. Diamond (Ithaca: Cornell University Press, 1976).
LPE 1993	'Notes for Lectures on "Private Experience" and "Sense Data"', edited and introduced by D. G. Stern, in J. C. Klagge und A. Nordmann (eds.), *Ludwig Wittgenstein. Philosophical Occasions 1912–1951* (Indianapolis and Cambridge, MA: Hackett, 1993), pp. 200–88.
LW 1992	*Last Writings on the Philosophy of Psychology / Letzte Schriften über die Philosophie der Psychologie,* vol. 2, edited by G. H. von Wright and H. Nyman, translated by C. G. Luckhardt and M. A. E. Aue (Oxford: Basil Blackwell, 1992).
LWL 1980	*Wittgenstein's Lectures: Cambridge, 1930–1932,* edited by D. Lee (Oxford: Basil Blackwell, 1980).
MAM 1958	Malcolm, N., *Ludwig Wittgenstein: A Memoir* (London: Oxford University Press, 1958).
MDC 1981	Drury, M. O'C., 'Conversations with Wittgenstein' in R. Rhees (ed.) *Recollections of Wittgenstein* (Oxford: Basil Blackwell, 1981), pp. 112–89.
MWL 1993	Moore, G. E., 'Wittgenstein's Lectures in 1930–33' in J. C. Klagge and A. Nordmann (eds.), *Ludwig Wittgenstein. Philosophical Occasions 1912–1951* (Indianapolis and Cambridge, MA: Hackett, 1993), pp. 45–114.
MWL 2016	Stern, D., *Wittgenstein: Lectures, Cambridge 1930–1933. From the Notes of G. E. Moore,* edited by D. Stern, B. Rogers and G. Citron (Cambridge: Cambridge University Press, 2016).
OC 1969	*On Certainty/Über Gewißheit,* edited by G. E. M. Anscombe and G. H. von Wright, translated by D. Paul and G. E. M. Anscombe (Oxford: Basil Blackwell, 1969).
PB 1964	*Philosophische Bemerkungen,* edited by Rush Rhees (Oxford: Basil Blackwell, 1964).
PB 1975	*Philosophical Remarks,* edited by Rush Rhees, translated by R. Hargreaves and R. White (Oxford: Basil Blackwell, 1975).

(cont.)

PG 1969	*Philosophische Grammatik*, edited by R. Rhees (Oxford: Basil Blackwell, 1969).
PG 1974	*Philosophical Grammar*, edited by R. Rhees, translated A. Kenny (Oxford: Basil Blackwell, 1974).
PGL 1988	*Wittgenstein's Lectures on Philosophical Psychology 1946–1947*, edited by P. T. Geach (New York: Harvester, 1988).
PI 1953	*Philosophical Investigations/Philosophische Untersuchungen*, edited by G. E. M. Anscombe and R. Rhees, translated by G. E. M. Anscombe (Oxford: Basil Blackwell, 1953).
PI 2009	*Philosophical Investigations/Philosophische Untersuchungen*, edited by P. M. S. Hacker and J. Schulte, translated by G. E. M. Anscombe, P. M. S. Hacker and Joachim Schulte (New York: Wiley, 2009).
PO 1993	*Philosophical Occasions 1912–1951*, edited and introduced by J. C. Klagge and A. Nordmann (Indianapolis and Cambridge, MA: Hackett, 1993).
PPO 2003	*Public and Private Occasions*, edited by J. C. Klagge and A. Nordmann (Lanham, Boulder, New York, Oxford: Rowman & Littlefield, 2003).
PT 1971	*Prototractatus. An Early Version of Tractatus Logico-Philosophicus*, edited by B. F. McGuinness, T. Nyberg and G. H. von Wright, with a translation by D. F. Pears and B. F. McGuinness, an historical introduction by G. H. von Wright and a facsimile of the author's manuscript (London: Routledge & Kegan Paul, 1971).
PU 2001	*Philosophische Untersuchungen. Kritisch-genetische Edition*, edited by J. Schulte in collaboration with H. Nyman, E. by Savigny and G. H. von Wright (Frankfurt am Main: Suhrkamp, 2001).
RFM 1956	*Remarks on the Foundations of Mathematics/ Bemerkungen über die Grundlagen der Mathematik*, edited by G. H. von Wright, R. Rhees and G. E. M. Anscombe, translated by G. E. M. Anscombe (Oxford: Basil Blackwell, 1956).

(cont.)

RFM 1974	*Bemerkungen über die Grundlagen der Mathematik,* edited by G. H. von Wright, R. Rhees and G. E. M. Anscombe, erweiterte und revidierte Neuausgabe (Frankfurt am Main: Suhrkamp, 1974).
RFM 1978	*Remarks on the Foundations of Mathematics/ Bemerkungen über die Grundlagen der Mathematik,* edited by G. H. von Wright, R. Rhees and G. E. M. Anscombe, translated by G. E. M. Anscombe, 3rd edition, revised and reset (Oxford: Basil Blackwell, 1978).
ROC 1977	*Remarks on Colour/Bemerkungen über die Farben,* edited by G. E. M. Anscombe, translated by L. L. McAlister and M. Schättle (Oxford: Basil Blackwell, 1977).
TB 1961	'Notebooks 1914–1916' in G. H. von Wright and G. E. M. Anscombe (eds.), translated by G. E. M. Anscombe, *Notebooks 1914–1916* (Oxford: Basil Blackwell, 1961), pp. 2–91.
TLP 1961	*Tractatus Logico-Philosophicus,* translated by D. F. Pears and B. F. McGuinness, International Library of Philosophy and Scientific Method (London: Routledge & Kegan Paul, 1961).
TLP 1989	*Logisch-philosophische Abhandlung. Tractatus Logico-Philosophicus,* edited by B. F. McGuinness and J. Schulte, Critical Edition (Frankfurt am Main: Suhrkamp, 1989).
VB 1977	*Vermischte Bemerkungen,* edited by G. H. von Wright in cooperation with H. Nyman (Frankfurt am Main: Suhrkamp, 1977).
VB 1980	*Culture and Value/Vermischte Bemerkungen,* edited by G. H. von Wright in cooperation with Heikki Nyman, translated by P. Winch, amended second edition (Oxford: Basil Blackwell, 1980).
VB 1994	*Vermischte Bemerkungen,* edited by G. H. von Wright in cooperation with H. Nyman, revised by A. Pichler (Frankfurt am Main: Suhrkamp, 1994).
VB 1998	*Vermischte Bemerkungen. Eine Auswahl aus dem Nachlaß/Culture and Value. A Selection from the Posthumous Remains,* edited by G. H. von Wright in

(cont.)

	cooperation with H. Nyman, revised by A. Pichler, translated by Peter Winch. Revised second edition. (Oxford: Blackwell 1998).
VW 2003	*The Voices of Wittgenstein. The Vienna Circle*, edited by G. Baker, translated by G. Baker, M. Mackert, J. Connolly and V. Politis (London, New York: Routledge, 2003).
WC 2008	*Wittgenstein in Cambridge. Letters and Documents, 1911–1951*, edited by B. F. McGuinness (Malden, MA: Blackwell, 2008).
WC 2012	*Wittgenstein in Cambridge. Letters and Documents, 1911–1951*, edited by B. F. McGuinness (Malden, MA: Blackwell, 2012).
WERKAUSGABE 1	*Werkausgabe Band 1. Tractatus Logico-Philosophicus /Tagebücher 1914–1916/Philosophische Untersuchungen* (Frankfurt am Main: Suhrkamp, 1984).
WERKAUSGABE 2	*Werkausgabe Band 2. Philosophische Bemerkungen* (Frankfurt am Main: Suhrkamp, 1984).
WERKAUSGABE 3	*Werkausgabe Band 3. Ludwig Wittgenstein und der Wiener Kreis* (Frankfurt am Main: Suhrkamp, 1984).
WERKAUSGABE 4	*Werkausgabe Band 4. Philosophische Grammatik* (Frankfurt am Main: Suhrkamp, 1984).
WERKAUSGABE 5	*Werkausgabe Band 5. Das Blaue Buch/Eine Philosophische Betrachtung (Das Braune Buch)* (Frankfurt am Main: Suhrkamp, 1984).
WERKAUSGABE 6	*Werkausgabe Band 6. Bemerkungen über die Grundlagen der Mathematik* (Frankfurt am Main: Suhrkamp, 1984).
WERKAUSGABE 7	*Werkausgabe Band 7. Bemerkungen über die Philosophie der Psychologie/Letzte Schriften über die Philosophie der Psychologie (Band 1)* (Frankfurt am Main: Suhrkamp, 1984).
WERKAUSGABE 8	*Werkausgabe Band 8. Bemerkungen über die Farben/ Über Gewißheit/Zettel/Vermischte Bemerkungen* (Frankfurt am Main: Suhrkamp, 1984).
Wi1	*Wiener Ausgabe Band 1*: Philosophische Bemerkungen (Vienna: Springer, 1994).

(cont.)

Wi2	*Wiener Ausgabe Band 2*: Philosophische Betrachtungen, Philosophische Bemerkungen (Vienna: Springer, 1994).
Wi3	*Wiener Ausgabe Band 3*: Bemerkungen, Philosophische Bemerkungen (Vienna: Springer, 1995).
Wi4	*Wiener Ausgabe Band 4*: Bemerkungen zur Philosophie, Bemerkungen zur philosophischen Grammatik (Vienna: Springer, 1995).
Wi5	*Wiener Ausgabe Band 5*: Philosophische Grammatik (Vienna: Springer, 1996).
Wi11	*Wiener Ausgabe Band 11:* The Big Typescript (Vienna: Springer, 2000) [TS 213].
WLP 1965	*Friedrich Waismann: The Principles of Linguistic Philosophy*, edited by R. Harré (London, New York: Macmillan/St. Martin's Press, 1965).
WLP 1976	*Friedrich Waismann: Logik, Sprache, Philosophie*, with a preface by M. Schlick, edited by G. P. Baker and B. McGuinness in collaboration with J. Schulte (Stuttgart: Philipp Reclam Jun, 1976).
WWK 1967	*Ludwig Wittgenstein und der Wiener Kreis*, edited by Brian McGuinness (Oxford: Basil Blackwell, 1967).
WWK 1979	*Ludwig Wittgenstein and the Vienna Circle*, conversations recorded by F. Waismann, edited by B. F. McGuinness, translated by J. Schulte and B. F. McGuinness (Oxford: Basil Blackwell, 1979).
YB 1979	'The Yellow Book (Selected Parts)' in A. Ambrose (ed.), *Wittgenstein's Lectures: Cambridge, 1932–1935* (Oxford: Basil Blackwell, 1979), pp. 41–73.
Z 1967	*Zettel / Zettel*, edited by G.E.M. Anscombe and G. H. von Wright (Oxford: Basil Blackwell, 1967).

The subsequent abbreviations used to refer to single pages or items in Wittgenstein's *Nachlass* follow the ones introduced by Wright, 'Wittgenstein Papers'. The assigned URL is the permanent web reference for each item or page to be accessed via wittgensteinsource.org.

Ms 101	www.wittgensteinsource.org/BFE/Ms-101_f
Ms 102	www.wittgensteinsource.org/BFE/Ms-102_f
Ms 103	www.wittgensteinsource.org/BFE/Ms-103_f
Ms 109	www.wittgensteinsource.org/BFE/Ms-109_f
Ms 114	www.wittgensteinsource.org/BFE/Ms-114_f
Ms 115	www.wittgensteinsource.org/BFE/Ms-115_f
Ms 117	www.wittgensteinsource.org/BFE/Ms-117_f
Ms 121	www.wittgensteinsource.org/BFE/Ms-121_f
Ms 122	www.wittgensteinsource.org/BFE/Ms-122_f
Ms 124	www.wittgensteinsource.org/BFE/Ms-124_f
Ms 125	www.wittgensteinsource.org/BFE/Ms-125_f
Ms 126	www.wittgensteinsource.org/BFE/Ms-126_f
Ms 127	www.wittgensteinsource.org/BFE/Ms-127_f
Ms 140	www.wittgensteinsource.org/BFE/Ms-140_f
Ms 142	www.wittgensteinsource.org/BFE/Ms-142_f
Ms 164	www.wittgensteinsource.org/BFE/Ms-164_f
Ms 169	www.wittgensteinsource.org/BFE/Ms-169_f
Ms 170	www.wittgensteinsource.org/BFE/Ms-170_f
Ms 171	www.wittgensteinsource.org/BFE/Ms-171_f
Ms 172	www.wittgensteinsource.org/BFE/Ms-172_f
Ms 173	www.wittgensteinsource.org/BFE/Ms-173_f
Ms 174	www.wittgensteinsource.org/BFE/Ms-174_f
Ms 175	www.wittgensteinsource.org/BFE/Ms-175_f
Ms 176	www.wittgensteinsource.org/BFE/Ms-176_f
Ms 177	www.wittgensteinsource.org/BFE/Ms-177_f
Ts 209	www.wittgensteinsource.org/BFE/Ts-209_f
Ts 213	www.wittgensteinsource.org/BFE/Ts-213_f
Ts 220	www.wittgensteinsource.org/BFE/Ts-220_f
Ts 221	www.wittgensteinsource.org/BFE/Ts-221_f
Ts 222	www.wittgensteinsource.org/BFE/Ts-222_f
Ts 223	www.wittgensteinsource.org/BFE/Ts-223_f
Ts 224	www.wittgensteinsource.org/BFE/Ts-224_f
Ts 225	www.wittgensteinsource.org/BFE/Ts-225_f
Ts 226	www.wittgensteinsource.org/BFE/Ts-226_f
Ts 309	www.wittgensteinsource.org/BFE/Ts-309-Stonborough_f
Ts 310	www.wittgensteinsource.org/BFE/Ts-310_f

Secondary Literature

Anscombe, G. E. M., 'Aristotle' in G. E. M. Anscombe and P. Geach, *Three Philosophers* (Oxford: Basil Blackwell, 1961), pp. 1–63.

Anscombe, G. E. M., *The Collected Philosophical Papers of G.E.M. Anscombe. Vol. II. Metaphysics and the Philosophy of Mind* (Oxford: Basil Blackwell, 1981).

Anscombe, G. E. M., *An Introduction to Wittgenstein's Tractatus* (London: Hutchinson, 1959).

Anscombe, G. E. M., *From Plato to Wittgenstein*, edited by M. Geach and L. Gormally (St Andrews: St Andrews Studies in Philosophy and Public Affairs, 2011).

Anscombe, G. E. M., 'Letter to the Editor', *Der Monat*, 43 (1952), 97–8.

Anscombe, G. E. M., 'The Reality of the Past' in M. Black (ed.), *Philosophical Analysis: A Collection of Essays* (Ithaca: Cornell University Press, 1950), 38–59.

Anscombe, G. E. M., Rhees, R. and von Wright, G. H., 'Note', *Mind*, 60 (1951), 584.

Bartley, W. W., *Wittgenstein* (London: Quartet Books, 1973).

Baum, W., *Wittgenstein im ersten Weltkrieg* (Vienna: Kitab-Verlag, 2014).

Broad, C. D., 'Hr. von Wright on the Logic of Induction (I–III)', *Mind*, 53 (1944), 1–24, 97–119, 193–214.

Broad, C. D., 'Review of Norman Malcolm. *Ludwig Wittgenstein: A Memoir*', *Universities Quarterly* (= *Higher Education Quarterly*), 13 (1959), 304–06.

Cranston, M., 'Bildnis eines Philosophen', *Der Monat*, 41 (1952), 495–7. Reprinted in: *Ludwig Wittgenstein: Schriften: Beiheft* (Frankfurt am Main: Suhrkamp, 1960), pp. 16–20.

Erbacher, C., '"Among the omitted stuff, there are many good remarks of a general nature" – On the Making of von Wright and Wittgenstein's *Culture and* Value', *Northern European Journal of Philosophy, SATS*, 18 (2) (2017), 79–113.

Erbacher, C., 'Brief aus Norwegen', *Deutsche Zeitschrift für Philosophie*, 65(3) (2017), 574–88.

Erbacher, C., 'Das Drama von Tübingen. Eine Humanities and Technology Story', *Working Paper Series Media of Cooperation*, 13 (2019), 1–42.

Erbacher, C., 'Editorial Approaches to Wittgenstein's *Nachlass*: Towards a Historical Appreciation', *Philosophical Investigations*, 38 (2015), 165–98.

Erbacher, C., '"Good" Philosophical Reasons for "Bad" Editorial Philology? On Rhees and Wittgenstein's *Philosophical Grammar*', *Philosophical Investigations*, 42(2) (2019), 111–145.

Erbacher, C., 'The Letters which Rush Rhees, Elizabeth Anscombe, and Georg Henrik von Wright Sent to Each Other', in T. Wallgren (ed.), *The Creation of Wittgenstein* (London: Bloomsbury, forthcoming).

Erbacher, C., 'Unser Denken bleibt gefragt: Web 3.0 und Wittgensteins Nachlass', in S. Windholz and W. Feigl (eds.), *Wissenschaftstheorie, Sprachkritik und Wittgenstein* (Heusenstamm: Ontos, 2011), 135–146.

Erbacher, C., 'Wittgenstein and his Literary Executors – Rush Rhees, Georg Henrik von Wright and Elizabeth Anscombe as Students, Colleagues and Friends of Ludwig Wittgenstein', *The Journal for the History of Analytical Philosophy*, 4(3) (2016), 1–39.

Erbacher, C., dos Santos Reis, A. and Jung, J., '"Ludwig Wittgenstein" – A BBC Radio Talk by Elizabeth Anscombe in May 1953', *Nordic Wittgenstein Review* 8(1–2) (2019), 225–40.

Erbacher, C., Jung, J. and Seibel, A., 'The Logbook of Editing Wittgenstein's *Philosophische Bemerkungen*', *Nordic Wittgenstein Review* 6(1) (2017), 105–47.

Erbacher, C. and Krebs, S. V., 'The First Nine Months of Editing Wittgenstein: Letters from G. E. M. Anscombe and R. Rhees to G. H. v. Wright', *Nordic Wittgenstein Review*, 4 (2015), 195–231.

Erbacher, C. and Schirmer, T., 'On Continuity: Rush Rhees on Outer and Inner Surfaces of Bodies', *Philosophical Investigations*, 39 (2016), 3–30.

Ferrater Mora, J., 'Wittgenstein oder die Destruktion', *Der Monat*, 41 (1952), 489–95. Reprinted in: *Ludwig Wittgenstein: Schriften: Beiheft* (Frankfurt am Main: Suhrkamp, 1960), pp. 21–9.

Gasking, D. A. T. and Jackson, A. C., 'Ludwig Wittgenstein', *Australasian Journal of Philosophy*, 29 (1953), 73–80.

Groddeck, W., Martens, G., Reuß and Straengle, P. 'Gespräch über die Bände 7 & 8 der Frankfurt Hölderlin-Ausgabe' *Text. Kritische Beiträge* 8 (2003), 1–55.

Ground, I. and Flowers III, F., *Portraits of Wittgenstein* (London: Bloomsbury Academic, 2015).

Hacker, P. and Baker, G., *Volume 1–4 of an Analytical Commentary in Philosophical Investigations* (Oxford: Wiley-Blackwell, 1980–1996).

Harrè, R., 'Gilbert Ryle and the *Tractatus*', *Linacre Journal*, 3 (1999), 39–53. www.linacre.ox.ac.uk/facilities/library/gilbert-ryle-collection

Hayek, F. A. v., *Friedrich August von Hayek's Draft Biography of Ludwig Wittgenstein: The Text and Its History* (Paderborn: Mentis, 2019).

Hintikka, J., 'An Impatient Man and His Papers', *Synthese*, 87(2) (1991), 183–201.

Hintikka, J., 'On Wittgenstein's 'Solipsism'', *Mind*, 67(265) (1958), 88–91.

Hölderlin, F., *Sämtliche Werke. Historisch-kritische Ausgabe in 20 Bänden und 3 Supplementen*, edited by D. E. Sattler (Frankfurt am Main, Basel: Stroemfeld/Roter Stern, 1975–2008).

Huitfeldt, C., 'Multi-Dimensional Texts in a One-Dimensional Medium', *Computers and the Humanities*, 28 (1995), 235–41.

Huitfeldt, C. 'Toward a Machine Readable Version of Wittgenstein's Nachlaß. Some Editorial Problems', in H. G. Senger (ed.), *Editio, 6, Philosophische Editionen* (Tübingen: Niemeyer, 1994), pp. 37–43.

Huitfeldt, C. and Rossvær, V., *The Norwegian Wittgenstein Project Report 1988* (Bergen: University of Bergen, 1988).

Janik, A., 'Remembering Kirchberg 1977', in C. Kanzian, V. Munz and S. Windholz (eds.), *Wir hofften jedes Jahr noch ein weiteres Symposium machen zu können. Zum 30. Internationalen Wittgenstein Symposium in Kirchberg am Wechsel* (Heusenstamm: Ontos, 2007), pp. 94–5.

Janik, A., *Wittgenstein's Vienna Revisited* (New Brunswick: Transaction Publishers, 2001).

Kenny, A., 'A Brief History of Wittgenstein Editing', in A. Pichler and S. Säätelä (eds.), *Wittgenstein: The Philosopher and His Works* (Heusenstamm: Ontos, 2005), 341–55.

Kenny, A., 'From the Big Typescript to the Philosophical Grammar', in J. Hintikka (ed.), *Essays on Wittgenstein in Honour of G. H. Von Wright, Acta Philosophica Fennica*, 28 (Helsinki: University of Helsinki, 1976),pp. 41–53.

Kenny, A., *A Life in Oxford* (London: John Murray, 1997).

Klagge, J., *Wittgenstein in Exile* (Cambridge, MA: MIT Press, 2011).

Klagge, J., 'The Wittgenstein Lectures, Revisited', *Nordic Wittgenstein Review*, 8(1+2) (2019), 11–82.

Kreisel, G., 'Wittgenstein's *Remarks on the Foundations of Mathematics*', *British Journal for the Philosophy of Science*, 9(34) (1958), 135–58.

Malcolm, N., 'Wittgenstein, Ludwig Josef Johann', in P. Edwards (ed.), *The Encyclopedia of Philosophy* (London: Macmillan Company and The Free Press, 1967), 327–40.

Maury, A., 'Sources of the Remarks in Wittgenstein's *Philosophical Investigations*', *Synthese*, 98 (1994), 349–78.

Maury, A., 'Sources of the Remarks in Wittgenstein's *Zettel*', *Philosophical Investigations*, 4 (1981), 57–74.

McGuinness, B. F., *Approaches to Wittgenstein: Collected Papers* (London: Routledge, 2002).

McGuinness, B. F., *Wittgenstein: A Life. Young Ludwig, 1889–1921* (London: Duckworth, 1988).

McGuinness, B. F., *Wittgenstein und Schlick* (Berlin: Parerga Verlag, 2010).

McGuinness, B. F. (ed.), *Moritz Schlick* (Heidelberg: Springer, 1985).

McGuinness, B. F. and Edwards-McKie, S., 'A Tapestry: Susan Edwards-McKie Interviews Professor Dr. B. F. McGuinness on the

Occasion of His 90th Birthday', *Nordic Wittgenstein Review*, 6(2) (2017), 85–90.

Monk, R., *Ludwig Wittgenstein – The Duty of Genius* (London: Vintage, 1991).

Moyal-Sharrock, D. (ed.), *The Third Wittgenstein. The Post-Investigations Works* (Aldershot: Ashgate, 2004).

Mühlhölzer, F., *Braucht die Mathematik eine Grundlegung? Ein Kommentar des Teils III von Wittgensteins Bemerkungen über die 'Grundlagen der Mathematik'* (Frankfurt am Main: Vittorio Klostermann, 2010).

Nedo, M., *Einführung in die Wiener Ausgabe* (Vienna: Springer, 1993).

New York Times, 'Radicalism of Rochester President's Son Causes Professor to Bar Youth from Class', 28 February 1924, 1.

Österman, B., '"He is a Perfect Nature-Being – and a Perfect Viennese!"': Von Wright and Wittgenstein in Cambridge 1939', in A. Siegetsleitner, A. Oberprantacher, and M-L. Frick (eds.), *Crisis and Critique: Philosophical Analysis and Current Events: 42nd International Wittgenstein Symposium. Kirchberg am Wechsel 4.-10. August 2019, Vol. 42* (Kirchberg am Wechsel, 2019), pp. 181–83.

Österman, B., 'Healing the Rift: How G. H. v. Wright made Philosophy Relevant to his Life', *Journal for the History of Analytical Philosophy*, 7(8) (2019), 1–18.

Paul, D., *Wittgenstein's Progress 1929–1951* (Bergen: Wittgenstein Archives, 2007).

Penrose, L. S. and Penrose, R., 'Impossible Objects: A Special Type of Visual Illusion', *British Journal of Psychology*, 49(1) (1958), 31–3.

Phillips, D. Z., 'Rush Rhees: A Biographical Sketch', in D. Z. Phillips (ed.), *Wittgenstein and the Possibility of Discourse*, 2nd edition (Malden, MA: Blackwell, 2006), pp. 266–75.

Pichler, A., *Untersuchungen zu Wittgensteins Nachlaß* (Bergen: Wittgenstein Archives, 1994).

Pichler, A., Biggs, M. A. R. and Szeltner, S. A., 'Bibliographie der deutsch- und englischsprachigen Wittgenstein-Ausgaben', *Wittgenstein-Studien*, 2 (2011), 249–86. www.ilwg.eu/files/Wittgenstein_Bibliographie.pdf. Accessed 27 August 2019.

Pichler, A. and Bruvik, T. M., 'Digital Critical Editing: Separating Encoding from Presentation', in D. Apollon, C. Belisle and P. Regnier (eds.), *Digital Critical Editions* (Champaign, IL: University of Illinois Press, 2014), pp. 179–99.

Pilch, M., 'Frontverläufe in Wittgenstein *Prototractatus*', *Wittgenstein-Studien*, 9(1) (2018), 101–54.

Potter, M., *Wittgenstein's Notes on Logic* (Oxford: Oxford University Press, 2011).

Ranchetti, M., *Lezioni e conversazioni sull'etica, l'estetica, la psicologia e la credenza religiosa*, edited by M. Ranchetti (Milan: Adelphi 1967).

Redpath, T., *Ludwig Wittgenstein: A Student's Memoir* (London: Duckworth, 1990).

Rhees, R., 'The *Tractatus*: Seeds of Some Misunderstandings', *Philosophical Review*, 72(2) (1963), 213–20.

Rhees, R., 'Wittgenstein', *The Human World*, 14 (1974), 66–78.

Rhees, R., *Wittgenstein's On Certainty. There – Like Our Lifes*, edited by D. Z. Phillips (Malden: Blackwell, 2003).

Rhees, R. (ed.), *Recollections of Wittgenstein* (Oxford: Oxford University Press, 1984).

Rinofner-Kreidl, S. and Wiltsche, H. A. (eds.), *Analytic and Continental Philosophy – Methods and Perspectives. Proceedings of the 37th International Wittgenstein Symposium* (Berlin: DeGruyter, 2016).

Rothhaupt, J., 'Wittgensteins "General Remarks"', *Wittgenstein-Studien*, 8 (2017), 103–36.

Schulte, J., 'Memories of Georg Henrik von Wright', in G. Meggle and R. Vilkko (eds.), 'Georg Henrik von Wright's book of friends', *Acta Philosophica Fennica*, 92 (2016), 187–202.

Schulte, J., 'Die Revision der englischen Übersetzung von Wittgensteins Philosophischen Untersuchungen. Ein Erfahrungsbericht', in M. Kroß and E. Ramharter (eds.), *Wittgenstein übersetzen* (Berlin: Parerga Verlag, 2012), pp. 173–94.

Schulte, J., 'Der Waismann-Nachlass', *Zeitschrift für Philosophische Forschung*, 33 (1976), 108–40.

Schulte, J., 'What Is a Work by Wittgenstein?', in A. Pichler and S. Säätelä (eds.), *Wittgenstein: The Philosopher and His Works* (Heusenstamm: Ontos, 2005), pp. 397–404.

Schulte, J., 'Wittgenstein's Last Writings', in S. Rinofner-Kreidl and H. A. Wiltsche (eds.), *Analytic and Continental Philosophy Methods and Perspectives. Proceedings of the 37th International Wittgenstein Symposium* (Berlin: De Gruyter, 2016), pp. 63–78.

Somavilla, I., 'Wittgenstein's Coded Remarks in the Context of His Philosophizing', in N. Venturinha (ed.), *Wittgenstein After His Nachlass* (Basingstoke: Palgrave Macmillan, 2010), pp. 30–59.

Stadler, F., *Studien zum Wiener Kreis. Ursprung, Entwicklung and Wirkung des Logischen Empirismus im Kontext* (Frankfurt am Main: Suhrkamp, 1997).

Stern, D., 'The Availability of Wittgenstein's Philosophy', in H. Sluga and D. Stern (eds.), *The Cambridge Companion to Wittgenstein* (Cambridge: Cambridge University Press, 1996), pp. 442–76.

Stern, D. G., 'How Many Wittgensteins?', in A. Pichler and S. Säätelä (eds.), *Wittgenstein: The Philosopher and His Works* (Heusenstamm: Ontos, 2005), pp. 164–88.

Teichmann, J. (2001). (Gertrude) Elizabeth Margaret Anscombe (1919–2001). *Oxford Dictionary of National Biography*. www.oxforddnb.com/. Accessed 10 December 2013.

Teichmann, R., *The Philosophy of Elizabeth Anscombe* (Oxford: Oxford University Press, 2008).

Toulmin, S. and Janik. A., *Wittgenstein's Vienna* (New York: Simon & Schuster, 1973).

Uffelmann, S., 'Vom System zum Gebrauch. Eine genetischphilosophische Untersuchung des Grammatikbegriffs bei Wittgenstein', in J. Conant, W., Kienzler, S. Majetschak, V. Munz, J. Rothaupt, D. Stern, and W. Vossenkuhl (eds.), *Über Wittgenstein*, 3 vols. (Berlin: De Gruyter, 2018), vol. 3.

Urmson, J. O., *Philosophical Analysis: Its Development Between the Two World Wars* (Oxford: Oxford University Press, 1956).

Westergaard, P., 'On the "Ketner and Eigsti Edition" of Wittgenstein's *Remarks on Frazer's The Golden Bough*', *Nordic Wittgenstein Review* 4(2) (2015), 117–42.

Wisdom, J., 'Philosophical Perplexity', *Proceedings of the Aristotelian Society*, 37 (1937), 71–88.

The Wittgenstein Archives at the University of Bergen, 'The Wittgenstein Archive at the University of Bergen: Annual Report 1995', *Working Papers from the Wittgenstein Archives at the University of Bergen*, No 12 (1996).

The Wittgenstein Archives at the University of Bergen, 'The Wittgenstein Archive at the University of Bergen: Project Report 1990–1993 and Critical Evaluation', *Working Papers from the Wittgenstein Archives at the University of Bergen*, No 9 (1995).

The Wittgenstein Archives at the University of Bergen, 'The Wittgenstein Archive at the University of Bergen: Background, Project Plan, and Annual Report 1990', *Working Papers from the Wittgenstein Archives at the University of Bergen*, No 2 (1991).

Wittgenstein, L., Rhees, R. and Citron, G. (eds.), 'Wittgenstein's Philosophical Conversations with Rush Rhees (1939–50): From the Notes of Rush Rhees' *Mind*, 142 (2015), 1–71.

Wright, G. H. v., 'Intellectual Autobiography' in P. A. Schilpp and L. E. Hahn (eds.), *The Philosophy of Georg Henrik von Wright, Volume 19* (La Salle, IL: Open Court, 1989), pp. 3–58.

Wright, G. H. v., 'Logistik filosofi', *Nya Argus*, 13 (1938), 175–7.

Wright, G. H. v., 'Ludwig Wittgenstein: A Biographical Sketch', *Philosophical Review*, 64 (1955), 527–45.

Wright, G. H. v., *Mitt Liv som jeg minns det* (Helsingfors: Söderström, 2001).

Wright, G. H. v., The Origin and Composition of Wittgenstein's *Investigations*, in C. G. Luckhardt (ed.), *Wittgenstein: Sources and Perspectives* (Ithaca, NY: Cornell University Press, 1979), pp. 138–60.

Wright, G. H. v., 'Special Supplement: The Wittgenstein Papers', *Philosophical Review*, 78(4) (1969), 483–503. Updates of the catalogue have been published in J. Klagge and A. Nordmann, *Ludwig Wittgenstein. Philosophical Occasions 1912–1951* (Indianapolis: Hackett Publishing Company, 1993), pp. 480–510.

Wright, G. H. v., 'The Troubled History of Part II of the *Investigations*', *Grazer Philosophische Studien*, 42 (1992), 181–92.

Wright, G. H. v., 'Über Wahrscheinlichkeit. Eine logische und philosophische Untersuchung', *Acta Societatis Scientiarum Fennicae Nova Series A*, 3(11) (1945).

Wright, G. H. v., *Wittgenstein* (Minneapolis: University of Minnesota Press, 1982).

Archival Material and Oral History Interviews

Anscombe, A., 'Correspondence with Rhees', Anscombe Archive at the University of Pennsylvania.

Documents archived by Peter Winch and succeeding secretaries to the board of trustees at the Wren Library at Trinity College Cambridge.

Heringer, J., 'Oral history interview', 23 March 2018, Erbacher personal archive.

Huitfeldt, C., 'Oral history interview', 27 August 2012, 18 June 2015, Erbacher personal archive.

Johannessen, H., 'Oral history interview', June 2015, Erbacher personal archive.

Kastil, A., 'Nachlass', Franz Brentano-Archiv at the University of Graz.

Kenny, A., 'Oral history interview', 27 March 2013, Erbacher personal archive.

Maury, A., 'Oral history interview', 26 September 2012, Erbacher personal archive.

McGuinness, B., 'Oral history interview', 20–3 October 2013, Erbacher personal archive.

Nedo, M., 'Oral history interview', 22–4 July 2015, Erbacher personal archive.

Nordenstam, T., 'Oral history interview', 15 December 2014, Erbacher personal archive.

Nowak, R., 'Documents related to the Wittgenstein Archive at the University of Tübingen', Nowak personal archive.

Nowak, R., 'Oral history interview', 23 May 2015, Erbacher personal archive.

Pichler, A. and Krüger, W., 'Oral history interview', 6 December 2013, Erbacher personal archive.

Rhees, R., 'Correspondence with Anscombe', Richard Burton Archive at the University of Swansea, UNI/SU/PC/1/1/3/2.

Rhees, R., 'Correspondence with Drury', Richard Burton Archive at the University of Swansea, UNI/SU/PC/1/1/3/4.

Rhees, R., 'Correspondence with Kenny', Richard Burton Archive at the University of Swansea, UNI/SU/PC/1/2/6/4.

Rhees, R., 'Correspondence with McGuinness', Richard Burton Archive at the University of Swansea, UNI/SU/PC/1/1/3/5.

'Rhees Papers' at the Wren Library at Trinity College Cambridge.

Rossvær, V., 'Oral history interview', 16–20 April 2018, Erbacher personal archive.

Wright, G. H. v., 'Correspondence with Anscombe', 1947–2001, National Library of Finland, COLL.714.11–12.

Wright, G. H. v., 'Correspondence with Kaila', National Library of Finland, COLL. 714.102–103

Wright, G. H. v., 'Correspondence with Kenny', National Library of Finland, COLL.714.110–111.

Wright, G. H. v., 'Correspondence with Malcolm', National Library of Finland, COLL.714.142–148.

Wright, G. H. v., 'Correspondence with McGuinness', National Library of Finland, 714.164.

Wright, G. H. v., 'Correspondence with Rhees', 1951–1967, 1989 NLF, COLL. 714.200–201.

Wright, G. H. v., 'Correspondence with Rhees', 1968–1988, Von Wright and Wittgenstein Archives at the University of Helsinki.

Acknowledgements

The research undergirding the book was funded by Nordforsk during the project *Joint Nordic Use of WAB Bergen and VWA Helsinki* (2010 and 2011), the Norwegian Research Council during the project *Shaping a domain of knowledge by editorial processing: the case of Wittgenstein's work* (NFR 213080, 2012–2015) and the German Research Foundation during the project *Medien der Kooperation*, TP P01: *Wissenschaftliche Medien der Praxistheorie: Harold Garfinkel und Ludwig Wittgenstein* (SFB 1187, 2016–2019). The Humboldt Foundation supported some parts of the work on this book through the *Research Center for Analytic German Idealism,* and so also did the Academy of Finland through the project *The Creation of Wittgenstein.*

I am grateful to the following libraries and archives for providing access to their holdings: the Drury Archive at the College Library Limerick, Franz Brentano-Archiv at the University of Graz, National Library of Finland, Richard Burton Archives at the University of Swansea, Von Wright and Wittgenstein Archives at the University of Helsinki, Wittgenstein Archives at the University of Bergen, Wren Library at Trinity College Cambridge, the preliminary Anscombe Archive and the private archives of Jürgen Heringer and Reinhard Nowak.

For granting permission to quote from letters, I thank the copyright holders Mrs M. C. Gormally (Dr Mary Geach) for Anscombe's letters, Anita and Benedict von Wright for von Wright's letters, and Volker Munz, the Richard Burton Archives and the Franz–Brentano Archive for Rhees's letters.

For sharing their memories and views in oral interviews, I thank James Conant, Nicholas Denyer, Cora Diamond, Mary Geach, Kevin Fitzpatrick, Luke Gormally, Ingrid Hänsel, Peter Hacker, Jürgen Heringer, Claus Huitfeldt, Tore Nordenstam, Allan Janik, Harald Johannessen, Anthony Kenny, André Maury, Michael Nedo, Franz Hespe, Ingolf Max, Brian McGuinness, Anselm Müller, Howard Mounce, Wilhelm Ott, Reinhard Nowak, Alois Pichler, Wilhelm Krüger, Viggo Rossvær, Mario von der Ruhr, Joachim Schulte, Peg Smythies, Pierre Stonborough, Anita von Wright and Benedict von Wright.

For decisive discussion, I am most grateful to James Conant, Allan Janik, Bernt Österman, Alois Pichler, Erhard Schüttpelz and Thomas Wallgren.

For help in copy editing and proofreading this book, I thank Arlyne Moi, Julia Jung, Anne dos Santos Reis and last but not least David Stern.

This book would not have been written were it not for my warm and inspiring conversations with Ralph Jewell.

Cambridge Elements ⹀

The Philosophy of Ludwig Wittgenstein

David G. Stern

University of Iowa

David G. Stern is a Professor of Philosophy and a Collegiate Fellow in the College of Liberal Arts and Sciences at the University of Iowa. His research interests include history of analytic philosophy, philosophy of language, philosophy of mind, and philosophy of science. He is the author of *Wittgenstein's Philosophical Investigations: An Introduction* (Cambridge University Press, 2004) and *Wittgenstein on Mind and Language* (Oxford University Press, 1995), as well as more than fifty journal articles and book chapters. He is the editor of *Wittgenstein in the 1930s: Between the 'Tractatus' and the 'Investigations'* (Cambridge University Press, 2018) and is also a co-editor of the *Cambridge Companion to Wittgenstein* (Cambridge University Press, 2nd edition, 2018), *Wittgenstein: Lectures, Cambridge 1930–1933, from the Notes of G. E. Moore* (Cambridge University Press, 2016) and *Wittgenstein Reads Weininger* (Cambridge University Press, 2004).

About the Series

This series provides concise and structured introductions to all the central topics in the philosophy of Ludwig Wittgenstein. The Elements are written by distinguished senior scholars and bright junior scholars with relevant expertise, producing balanced and comprehensive coverage of the full range of Wittgenstein's thought.

Cambridge Elements ≡

The Philosophy of Ludwig Wittgenstein

Elements in the Series

Wittgenstein's Heirs and Editors
Christian Erbacher

A full series listing is available at: www.cambridge.org/EPLW